# THE GREAT GARLIC COOKBOOK

# THE
# GREAT GARLIC
## COOKBOOK

**BARBARA FRIEDLANDER MEYER**
**AND**
**BOB CATO**

M. Evans & Company, Inc.
New York

M. Evans and
Company, Inc.
216 East 49th Street
New York, New York
10017

Manufactured in the
United States of America

9 8 7 6 5 4 3 2 1

Library of Congress
Cataloging-in-Publication
Data

Meyer, Barbara Friedlander,
1934-
    The great garlic cookbook
    / by Barbara Friedlander
    and Bob Cato.
        p. cm.
    Includes index.
    ISBN 0-87131-673-0 :
    $14.95
    1. Cookery (Garlic)
    I. Cato, Bob.   II. Title
TX819.G3M48   1991
641.6′526—dc20 91-43496
                    CIP

## ACKNOWLEDGMENTS

Many thanks to: Carlos Anduze, Andrea Bankoff, Jonathan Cott, Marcia Davis, Tony Heilbut, Pepe Lopez Colmenar, Marilyn Petersen, Paul Price, Louis Savas, and Barbara's mother, Jessie Bankoff, and Bob's mother, Ysabel Maddox.

# CONTENTS

# INTRODUCTION

Garlic! The very name elicits a strong response; laughs or grimaces, joy or repugnance, no herb has a history marked with such reverence and such disdain. Garlic is one of the most ancient cultivated plants, probably originally from western Asia and grown in China over 6,000 years ago. The Egyptians cultivated it on a large scale, and it was of such importance there that one could swear oaths upon it. The Hebrews, glad to leave their bondage in Egypt, nevertheless mourned certain losses: "We remember the fish which we did eat in Egypt freely . . . and the onions and the garlick" (Numbers 11:5). Roman soldiers ate garlic to make them more courageous and dedicated the plant to Mars, the god of war. The upper classes throughout history have generally scorned it as food and yet garlic was a staple in the diet of the common man.

However, it was less as food and more as medicine that garlic achieved its early notoriety. Possibly man's first antibiotic, garlic was found to cure (or at least alleviate) a wide spectrum of ailments. Probably for this reason it was surrounded by superstition and myth. After all, what is illness if not a demon? The section in this book called "The Garlic Medicine Chest" briefly covers this use of garlic. In describing the various treatments, the authors make no claims or implications for garlic as a remedy.

Botanically, *allium sativum* is a member of the lily family—an unlikely geneology until one compares its white or purple flowers with a lily's. (A wreath of garlic flowers was worn by one of his victims in an attempt to ward off the vampire in the book *Dracula*.) The garlic bulb or head is a composite of several small cloves covered by a thin paper-like skin. There are many varieties and bulbs vary in size and number of cloves, as well as pungency. It is well to note this when following a recipe, as the garlic referred to here is medium-sized. Ultimately, your individual taste will determine the quantity to use.

Today, thankfully, garlic contributes a unique flavor to as many gourmet dishes as provincial ones. The major objection is still its odor, but chlorophyll and green herbs can usually minimize that. Besides, many people feel it's worth the consequences. We happen to be among those enthusiastic proponents of this "super bulb."

Although Barbara is a vegetarian and natural foods "addict," in order to include a large and important category of recipes, Bob has created and tested the meat, poultry and fish dishes. Good eating!

**66** Garlic all powerful; marvelous seasoning; you are the essence, the incense which revives and exhilarates; you are the spur that excites, stimulates. Garlic! You stir up, you impel, you cheer; you are the only condiment, you are the glorious one, the sovereign extract of the earth. **99**

GUSTAVE COQUIOT

## SOME TIPS ON BUYING, STORING AND USING GARLIC

Try to buy large, fat, hard bulbs which have not pulled away from their paperlike coverings; bulbs that show no discoloration (if there is discoloration, make sure to cut it all away). Store garlic in a dry place.

Garlic is two-faced—a gentle seasoning when used whole, a forceful, potent and intrusive taste the more it is mashed, minced or cut. And raw garlic always speaks louder than cooked. When one eats garlic-drowned dishes on a steady basis, it is possible to destroy the taste buds, which, when exposed to strong attack, become immune to delicate flavors.

Rubbing a bowl with a clove of raw garlic gives a whiff to a salad. For slightly more pungency, rub a clove against the point of a fork tine; for a lot more, hit the clove sharply with a knife and then begin chopping.

The most discreet way to use garlic in a salad is to make what the French call a *chapon*— a dry piece of bread that is rubbed all over with cut garlic and then tossed lightly with the greens and dressing. The extreme of discretion would be to follow the example of Queen Victoria's chef: chew a clove of garlic and then breathe over the salad immediately before serving! It is well to remember that the longer garlic rests in a dressing or sauce the stronger the taste will be; fifteen minutes is usually the maximum time if you're aiming for subtlety.

10

In cooking, if you want to keep garlic under control, do not mince it. Instead, cut the clove in half lengthwise. If you're even more cautious, stick the halves with a toothpick, cook them with the food for no more than a half hour and remove them.

Garlic browns quickly and burns easily; make sure oil is not too hot and remove garlic quickly from deep-frying, high-temperature dishes.

Peeling garlic is never easy. It will help if you hold the point of the clove, concave side down, against a plate and squash it gently with your thumb. The clove should pull away easily from its covering. If you tear readily, garlic can be as lethal as onion. Some of this can be avoided by sitting upright and extending your arms (the idea is to stay as far away as possible).

What to do about your fingers: using a press or crushing the cloves between several pieces of waxed paper with a rolling pin will help keep your fingers smell-free. If you do happen to get garlic on your hands, rub them with a little salt and rinse them in cold water.

# GREAT GARLIC RECIPES

**66** Here capers a sauce vermilion
Whose fragrant odors to the soul are blown.
Here pungent garlic meets the eager sight
And whets with savor sharp the appetite. . . . **99**

Written in ecstasy by a poet of Baghdad
about a tray of hors d'oeuvres.

# Appetizers

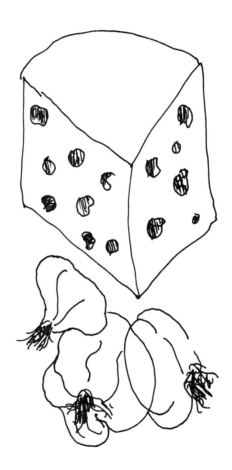

## RUSSIAN GARLIC MARROW

*What to do on a cold night: Eat this with vodka*

marrow bones
many cloves garlic, crushed
much fresh ground pepper

1. Cook the bones well and remove marrow.
2. Mash marrow, garlic and pepper, and spread on pieces of black bread.

## HEALTHY AND HOT SANDWICH SPREAD

1 cup tahini (sesame paste)
2 tablespoons tamari (soy sauce)
3 cloves garlic, crushed
apple cider vinegar
sprouts (bean or alfalfa) or pimiento for garnish

Blend all ingredients, adding enough vinegar for a creamy consistency. Spread on slices of bread and top with sprouts or pimiento.

# GUACAMOLE (AVOCADO DIP)

salt
2 or more cloves garlic, sliced
4 avocados
2 onions, chopped fine or grated
2 tomatoes, blanched, peeled and chopped
    fine
1 tablespoon lemon juice
2 teaspoons chili powder
1 tablespoon mayonnaise (optional)

1. Salt the bottom of a bowl and rub
garlic into the salt.
2. Mash avocados well into bowl and combine
with onions and tomatoes.
3. Add lemon juice, salt to taste, chili powder
and a thin coating of mayonnaise.

NOTE

If a stronger garlic flavor is desired, crush
cloves instead of rubbing them in salt.

## HUMUS DIP

*This is a purée of chick peas and is designed to be used as a dip with taco chips or some equivalent. It can be converted into a spread by decreasing the amount of liquid and blending more coarsely.*

2 cups chick peas, soaked 6 to 8 hours and
     cooked until tender in lots of water
4 tablespoons tahini (sesame paste)
juice of 3 lemons
4 cloves garlic, crushed
olive oil
salt and pepper to taste

1. Combine chick peas, tahini, lemon juice, garlic and enough cooking water for a consistency of a dip.
2. Add enough olive oil for a creamy consistency, salt and pepper.
3. Serve cold, garnished with chopped parsley.

## BEA'S BULBS

*For the real garlic lover, there's no limit!*

1 pound mushrooms
up to two bulbs of garlic, peeled
French dressing

Chop mushrooms and garlic together as finely as possible, add enough French dressing to moisten and serve chilled with toasted bread squares or crackers.

# SPIEDINI FOR LEO LIONNI

serves 6

*This is a hot cheese and anchovy appetizer.*

 1 loaf Italian bread
 1 pound mozzarella cheese
½ cup melted butter
 3 tablespoons olive oil
½ cup chopped anchovies
 1 clove garlic, minced
¼ teaspoon freshly ground pepper
 2 tablespoons minced parsley
 3 tablespoons wine vinegar

1. Preheat oven to 400°.
2. Cut bread into slices about ½-inch thick and trim off crusts.
3. Cut slices into 1½-inch squares. Cut cheese the same size.
4. Place bread and cheese alternately on six skewers, beginning and ending with bread. Brush on all sides with melted butter.
5. Bake for 10 minutes or until browned. Turn skewers often to brown all sides.
6. While the Spiedini is baking, heat oil in a sauce pan, add anchovies and garlic and stir until anchovies are practically dissolved.
7. Add pepper, parsley and vinegar, and pour sauce over the Spiedini.

# EGGPLANT CAPONATA

serves 6–8

   1 medium eggplant, peeled and cut into
      cubes
   6 tablespoons olive oil
   2 cloves garlic, minced
   1 onion, sliced thin
 ¾ cup chopped celery
   4 tablespoons tomato sauce
2½ tablespoons capers
  14 stuffed green olives, cut in half
   1 tablespoon sugar (optional)
   2 tablespoons wine vinegar
   salt and freshly ground pepper to taste

1. Sauté eggplant in 5 tablespoons oil.
2. Remove eggplant onto plate, add last
   spoon of oil to frying pan and gently sauté
   garlic and onion until golden brown.
3. Add celery and tomato sauce, and simmer
   until celery is tender.
4. Add eggplant, capers and olives.
5. In a separate pan heat sugar and vinegar,
   and pour over eggplant mixture. Add salt
   and pepper and simmer for an additional
   15 minutes, stirring frequently.
6. Serve hot or cold with toast or crackers;
   or add to a salad.

NOTE

For a smoother caponata, let it cool and then
use the blender.

# GUACAMUNGI

serves 4

2 ripe avocados
4 cloves garlic, crushed
juice of 1 lemon
dash of tamari (soy sauce)
salt to taste
pinch each of oregano, parsley, thyme
½ cup mung bean sprouts

1. Mash avocados and garlic together.
2. Mix in other ingredients and blend well.
3. Serve on toast, crackers or toasted
   seaweed strips.

## ERIC'S SATURDAY AFTERNOON SANDWICH

1 long loaf French or Italian bread
2 cloves garlic, split
1 2-ounce can flat anchovies
6 large black pitted olives
1 cucumber, peeled and sliced thin
1 tomato, sliced thin
3 pimientos, cut in half
1 medium onion, sliced thin
salt and pepper
olive oil
vinegar

1. Cut bread lengthwise and rub the inside of both halves with garlic.
2. Place anchovies, olives, cucumber, tomato, pimientos and onion on one half. Sprinkle with salt, pepper, oil and vinegar.
3. Press sandwich together and place something heavy on top of it for about a half hour.
4. When ready to serve, slice into sandwiches.

# SHRIMP AND MUSHROOM APPETIZER

serves 4–6

for Joel Grey and His Dear Lady Wife, Jo

  1 pound firm white mushrooms
  ¼ teaspoon minced garlic
  ½ cup olive oil
  ½ teaspoon freshly ground pepper
  4 tablespoons lemon juice
  1 pound shrimp, cooked and cleaned
1¼ teaspoon salt

1. Wash and dry mushrooms well. Remove stems (which can be saved and used for soups or sauces).
2. Slice mushroom caps paper thin and combine with garlic, oil, pepper and lemon juice. Marinate in refrigerator for 1 hour, turning frequently.
3. One half hour before serving, add shrimp and salt.

## PEPPER APPETIZER

A Hot Shot for Bob Dylan

   3 cloves garlic, sliced thin
1½ cups fresh tomatoes, peeled and cubed
 ½ cup anchovies, minced
   3 tablespoons dry bread crumbs
   3 tablespoons olive oil
   6 green and red peppers mixed; or all
        green or red
   4 tablespoons butter

1. Preheat oven to 375°.
2. Combine garlic, tomatoes, anchovies,
   bread crumbs and oil.
3. Cut peppers in quarters lengthwise;
   remove core and seeds.
4. Fill peppers with garlic mixture and place
   in an oiled baking pan; dot with butter.
5. Bake for 30 minutes.
6. Chill and serve cold.

## FELAFEL

yield: at least 20

*This is a spicy delicious filling made to order for the pouch in Middle Eastern bread (Pita).*

2 cups dried chick peas, soaked 6 to 8 hours
1 large onion, chopped fine
2 cloves garlic, crushed
handful of parsley, chopped fine
2 teaspoons ground cumin
1 teaspoon ground coriander
½ teaspoon chili powder or small chili
    pepper, chopped fine
salt to taste
cayenne pepper to taste
½ teaspoon baking powder or yeast
vegetable or peanut oil
lettuce
cucumbers
tomatoes
green peppers
hot sauce (chili powder and mayonnaise
or tahini and yogurt)
bread

1. Put peas through a meat grinder and mix with all remaining ingredients, up to oil.
2. Mince and pound into a fine paste; allow to stand for about 15 minutes.
3. Heat oil very hot in a frying pan, form felafel mixture into small flat cakes and deep fry until golden brown on all sides. Drain.
4. Chop up lettuce, cucumbers, tomatoes and green peppers.
5. Make the hot sauce.
6. Spoon into each small bread 2 or 3 felafel and enough salad to fill; top it all off with hot sauce.

## HOT DIP FOR TOM WILSON

*For raw vegetables.*

5 cloves garlic, sliced thin
¼ pound butter
¼ cup olive oil
½ cup anchovies, chopped fine

1. Combine garlic, butter and oil and cook over low heat or in double boiler for 15 minutes. Do not boil.
2. Add anchovies and mix until almost dissolved.
3. Remove from fire and keep warm in a chafing dish.

Use as a dip for raw vegetables such as celery, carrots, cauliflower, cucumber and endive.

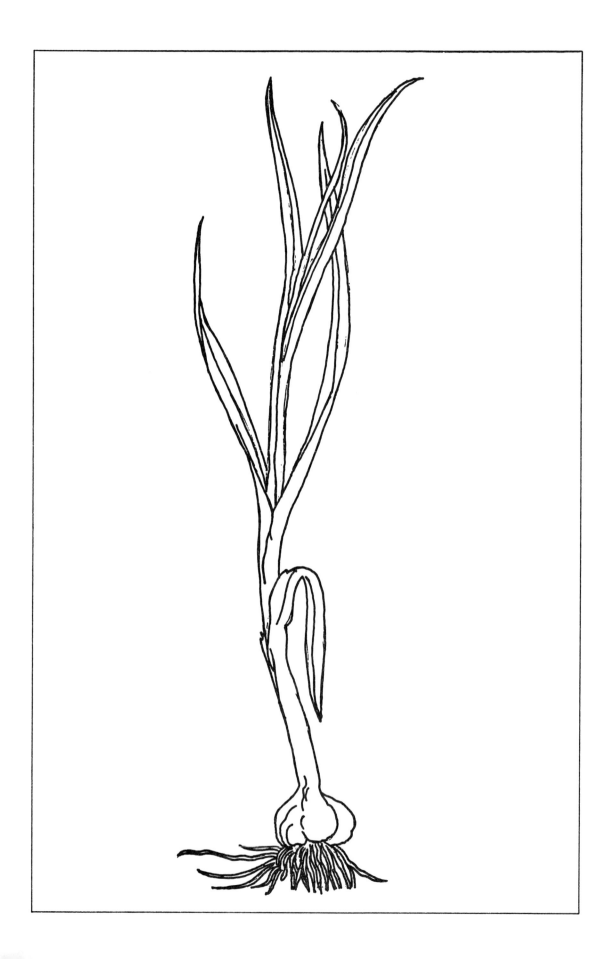

## FARCE D'AIL

*This "farce" can be a match for the meanest martini.*

6 hard-boiled egg yolks
6 cloves garlic, blanched
2 tablespoons butter

1. Mash egg yolks and garlic together.
2. Add butter and cream well.
3. Put mixture through a sieve and serve with crackers or toasted French bread squares.

## PÂTÉ MAISON

1 cup solidly packed raw chicken (or turkey) and raw veal
1 clove garlic, cut in half
1 shallot, peeled and cut in half
½ cup solidly packed raw bacon
½ cup solidly packed prosciutto
pinch each of salt, pepper and cinnamon
1 egg
1 tablespoon brandy
1 bay leaf

1. Preheat oven to 400°.
2. Meanwhile in a blender, food grinder or processor (if using a processor, use the steel knife), mix chicken, veal, garlic and shallot until fine.
3. Add remaining ingredients (except bay leaf) and grind everything until mixture is smooth and the ham finely chopped.
4. Place in a two-cup tureen with bay leaf on top and bake 40 minutes or until pâté pulls away from sides and is brown on top.
5. Cover and refrigerate. Serve with crusty French bread.

**66** The World's affection is not
devoid of malice; it has 'garlic in
the almond-cake.' **99**

JALALU'DDIN RUMI

## CARLOS' GARLIC BREAD

*Carlos says that Cubans love to eat this for breakfast but those who are less adventurous may prefer it a bit later in the day.*

½ cup olive oil
2 tablespoons sesame oil
1 bulb garlic, unpeeled and crushed
3 shallots, unpeeled and crushed
1 loaf Italian or French bread

1. Heat combined oils and fry garlic and shallots until golden.
2. Strain oil, discarding garlic and shallots.
3. Spread oil on bread or fry bread in strained oil.

## RAW AND RUGGED GARLIC CROUTONS

*Toss this in your favorite green salad.*

Rub crusts from old bread with garlic cloves. Mix together with a dressing of oil, vinegar, salt and pepper.

**66** Wel loved he garleek, onyons and eek lekes,
And for to drinken strong wyn, reed as blood. **99**

CHAUCER, *Canterbury Tales*

# Sauces

## SKORTHALIA: THE GREEKS' WORD FOR IT

*This is a potent garlic sauce for fish or vegetables which can also be served as a dry dip.*

  7 cloves garlic, crushed
  3 potatoes, boiled in their skins, peeled and
      mashed
  1 cup olive oil
⅓ cup vinegar or lemon juice
  salt and pepper to taste

1. Mash the garlic and potatoes together until mixture is smooth.
2. Slowly add, alternately, oil and vinegar or lemon juice.
3. Add seasoning and whip until stiff. Thin, if desired, with chicken or fish broth or hot water.

Sauce may be refrigerated for later use.

VARIATIONS

Any of the following may be added: avocado, tahini (sesame paste), crushed almonds, walnuts or pignoli.

# TWO NUTTY GARLIC RECIPES

A SAUCE

1 cup shelled walnuts, chopped
2 cloves garlic, cut
¼ cup olive oil
 salt to taste
 pinch of foenugreek powder

1. Grind walnuts and garlic into a paste either
   in a mortar and pestle or an electric
   grinder.
2. Gradually add olive oil and stir well until
   you achieve desired consistency; add
   seasonings.

AN APPETIZER

3 cloves garlic, sliced
2 tablespoons butter or oil
2 cups shelled almonds or cashews, whole
      or cut in half
salt

1. Brown garlic slowly in butter or oil; then
   remove garlic.
2. Toast nuts in pan until butter or oil is
   totally absorbed and nuts are lightly
   browned; salt and serve with drinks.

## THE SIMPLEST GARLIC OIL

To make a useful salad or cooking oil with a delicate garlic flavor, peel as many cloves as you like for a quart of good oil. Do not cut them but let them remain in the oil for several hours or even better overnight. Remove them; store the oil in a cool place and use as desired.

## NEVER ENOUGH SAUCE

2 onions, chopped fine
4 cloves garlic, chopped fine
1 tablespoon oil
water
1 tablespoon tahini (sesame paste)
dash of tamari (soy sauce)

1. Sauté onions and garlic in oil until starting to brown.
2. Heat a small amount of water and dilute tahini in it to make a creamy white sauce.
3. Add onion-garlic mixture and tamari. Mix well and serve warm as a dip for raw vegetables such as cauliflower, broccoli, Jerusalem artichokes, carrot and celery sticks.

# GARLIC BUTTER

*This butter is used mostly for steaks and hot breads.*

8 cloves garlic
½ cup butter, at room temperature
chopped parsley

1. Steam cloves in water until partially soft; then drain.
2. Crush cloves with garlic press or spoon, and combine with butter.
3. Strain through a fine sieve and add parsley.

# AL AJILLO

*This is a marvelous method Spaniards use to cook a variety of dishes in garlic-flavored oil.*

¼ cup oil
   3 or 4 cloves garlic, cut horizontally in thick
     slices
   2 pounds mushrooms, tomatoes, peppers,
     onions or other quick-cooking items
   hot red pepper, crushed (optional)
   salt to taste

1. Heat oil in a large heavy frying pan or wok; when oil is very hot, add garlic.
2. Fry over medium heat for a few minutes until slightly soft and starting to brown; add vegetables.
3. Mix garlic, vegetables and red pepper, and sauté for a few minutes; add salt.
4. Turn heat off, cover, and allow vegetables to finish cooking. Serve immediately.

VARIATIONS

For shrimp, mussels, baby eels, clams or steamers:

1. Allow garlic to brown first; add fish, stir, cover and cook over low heat until finished. Serve immediately.

For slower cooking items such as chicken and rabbit:

1. Fry garlic in oil until brown; remove garlic, add ingredients, cover and cook until tender. Serve immediately and garnish with the garlic slices.

# GARLIC MAYONNAISE

yield: 1½ cups

  1 cup olive oil
  1 egg
½ teaspoon salt
½ teaspoon dry mustard
  2 tablespoons lemon juice
  3 cloves garlic

1. Put ¼ cup oil, egg, salt, mustard and lemon juice in blender and blend at low speed for a few minutes.
2. Add remaining oil and continue blending until mixture has reached the consistency of mayonnaise.
3. Add garlic cloves and blend for about 10 seconds.

This mayonnaise may be used on hot or cold fish, meat and vegetables.

## OLÉ GARLIC MAYONNAISE

(Spanish: *All y Oli;* French: *Aioli*)

yield: 1 cup

10 cloves garlic
 1 cup oil
 salt to taste
 juice of 1 lemon (optional)

1. Using a mortar and pestle, crush garlic
   cloves into paste.
2. Add oil very gradually, turning pestle in
   one direction only.
3. Continue turning until mixture is the
   consistency of thick mayonnaise. Add salt
   and lemon. Refrigerate.

Serve cold on meat, fish or cold potatoes,
garnish with parsley.

## SAUCE CATALANE FOR GRILLED MEATS

1 onion, chopped fine
diced ham (optional)
1 tablespoon oil
flour
1 cup water
1 cup white wine
12 cloves garlic, sliced
1 lemon, sliced
¾ cup almonds

1. Sauté onion and ham in oil until golden.
2. Sprinkle in a bit of flour to thicken slightly.
3. Add water and wine, and stir well until smooth.
4. Add garlic and lemon; cover and simmer over low heat for a half hour.
5. Crush almonds in a mortar or electric grinder and stir into sauce 5 minutes before serving. Serve hot.

## TURKISH YOGURT

yield: 2 quarts

6 cloves garlic, crushed
salt and pepper to taste
1 tablespoon cider or wine vinegar
1 cucumber, chopped fine
2 quarts yogurt

1. Combine garlic, salt, pepper and vinegar.
2. Add cucumber and yogurt; mix well and
   chill for at least an hour.

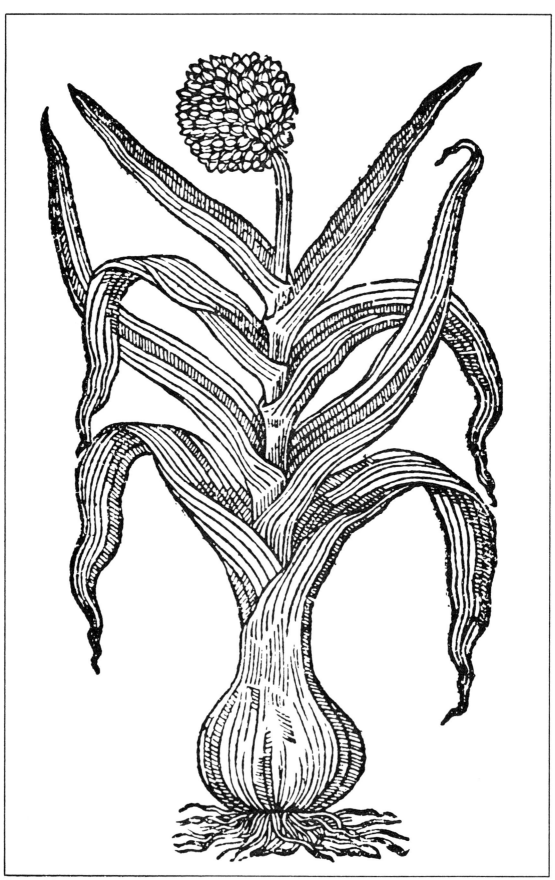

Great Mountain garlic, 16th century woodcut

# BOB'S BASIL AND TOMATO SAUCE

yield: approx. 3 cups

*It's worth all the time it takes.*

 4 tablespoons olive oil
 2 onions, sliced thin
 3 cloves garlic, minced
 3 stalks celery, chopped
 1 carrot, sliced
15 or more leaves of fresh basil
 1 cup tomato puree
 1 large (1 lb. 3 oz.) can tomatoes
 1 cup water
 2 bay leaves
½ teaspoon oregano

1. Heat oil in pan, add onion and garlic and sauté until onions are wilted but not yet brown.
2. Add remaining ingredients; partially cover pan and simmer for 3 hours.
3. Put mixture through a food mill and cook an additional 2 hours.

## MARVELOUS MARINARA
## FOR MITCH MILLER

yield: approx. 3 cups

  2 cloves garlic, sliced thin
½ cup chopped onion
¼ cup olive oil
  4 cups canned tomatoes
½ cup fresh chopped parsley
½ teaspoon oregano
  4 whole fresh basil leaves or 1 teaspoon
      dried basil
salt and pepper to taste

1. Sauté garlic and onions in oil until golden brown.
2. Add all other ingredients and simmer until thickened—about 1 hour. If a smoother sauce is desired, put tomatoes through a food mill.

# GARLIC LOVERS' PESTO GENOVESE

yield: 2 cups

*The best thing to ever meet spaghetti, pesto can be added to minestrone. Result: Minestrone Genovese!*

12 cloves garlic, chopped
20 large basil leaves (basil must be fresh)
12 tablespoons freshly grated Parmesan
    cheese
⅔ cup pine nuts or walnut meats
 2 sprigs fresh parsley
½ teaspoon salt
½ cup olive oil

1. Use a blender or mortar and pestle to crush, mix and blend garlic, basil, cheese, nuts, parsley and salt into a paste.
2. Add oil gradually and continue blending until smooth.
3. Serve over hot pasta with a lump of butter and some more freshly grated Parmesan cheese.

NOTE

If refrigerating or freezing pesto, add a topping of olive oil. There's no need to warm it to room temperature when serving. Just make sure the pasta is hot.

Lamb and garlic have been happily wedded for ages: In China, circa 600 B.C., the spring rites included the sacrifice of a lamb which was seasoned with aromatics and garlic before it was cooked over wood.

## GARLIC ON THE LAMB

yield: 1½–2 cups

*A sauce for lamb*

1 large bulb garlic, separated into cloves
    and peeled
1 cup water
¼ teaspoon salt
¼ teaspoon rosemary
 pinch of thyme
2 tablespoons raw bulgur wheat (rice may
    be substituted)
1 cup brown stock, lamb or beef
¼ cup dry red wine

1. Steam garlic cloves until tender but not mushy; drain.
2. Meanwhile, combine water, salt, herbs and bulgur, and cook over low heat for 10 minutes.
3. Add garlic and simmer slowly for a half hour, or until bulgur is cooked.
4. Add stock and wine, and simmer for about 1 minute.
5. Allow to cool slightly, then put in blender and blend until smooth. Add more boiling water if sauce is too thick and adjust seasonings to taste.
6. When lamb is ready, strain the juice, add to sauce and reheat. Serve hot over lamb.

# SUPERSTITIONS, MYTHS AND MAGIC

"He who wears a clove of garlic need not fear the evil eye."    Ancient Chinese saying

In doorways from Bangalore to Transylvania, garlic was hung to keep out vampires and other demons. In fact, in Sanskrit its name actually means "slayer of monsters."

Wild garlic (the moly plant) was given to Ulysses by Mercury so that he and his men might withstand the wiles and charms of Circe.

The ancient Greeks placed bulbs of garlic on top of the piles of stone which denoted cross-roads to provide a supper for Hecate; what better way to stay on the good side of a goddess from the netherworld?

The Roman, Pliny, believed a magnet would become powerless if brought into close contact with garlic.

Bull fighters in South America have been known to wear a garlic clove around their necks to prevent a bull from charging.

Palestinian grooms would wear a clove as a boutonniere to insure a happy wedding night.

Garlic plays an important role in holophrastic magic where particular personal items are used for charms or hexes. For a simple love charm, two garlic bulbs are punctured with a steel nail which is left inside to hold both bulbs together. The top bulb represents the individual making the charm and the bottom bulb represents the desired lover. The charm is hidden in the corner of a dark closet until the one he cares for begins to respond. This garlic charm is said to make a lover overflow with passion.

50

Recipe for warding off evil: If you know of someone who is trying to cross or hex you, it is a relatively easy matter to avert the oncoming evil. Blend the following ingredients in your bathwater: garlic, 7 small pieces; a pinch of thyme; 7 dry basil leaves; 7 can shakes each of parsley flakes and sage; 7 drops of geranium oil; and a pinch of saltpeter. Carefully mix the above items and use for a protective bath on Tuesday, Thursday and Saturday. After bathing for 14 minutes, dry off completely and rub down thoroughly with bay rum. Follow with a second rubdown using verbena perfume oil. This procedure is said to uncross any hexed person and also prevents them from being hexed for a period of 7 weeks.

(Interestingly enough: an herbal recipe for general purification involves 1 whole garlic bulb and 1 ounce of thyme boiled in at least 5 gallons of water for 1 hour and put in a bath of hot water. Garlic when used this way does not leave an odor but has the reverse effect of deodorizing.)

Garlic is believed to turn away spirits of the dead and protect an individual from all evil. Pieces of garlic are placed in a small cloth sack and tied around the neck as a powerful voodoo charm. Use red flannel when possible. (Some Arabs carry blue velvet cushions with garlic cloves inside to ward off evil.)

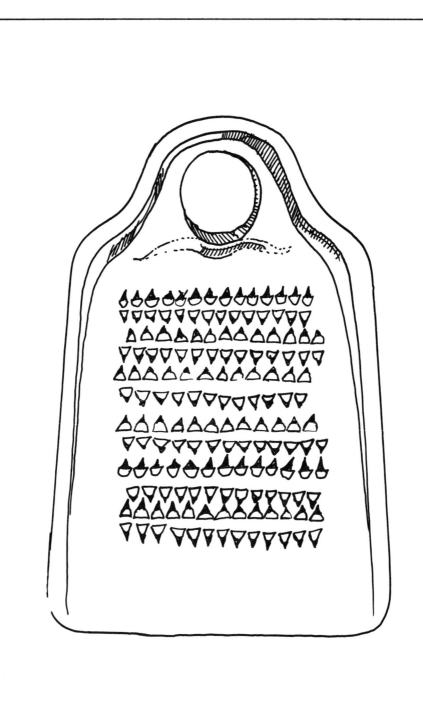

Japanese porcelain garlic (or ginger) grater

# Pasta

15th century woodcut

# AMAGANSETT CLAM SAUCE AND SPAGHETTI

serves 4–6

  1 pound clams, scrubbed clean
¾ cup olive oil
  3 cloves garlic, crushed
1½ pounds tomatoes, peeled
    salt and pepper to taste
  ¼ cup chopped parsley
  1 pound spaghetti, cooked *al dente*

1. Place clams in a pan with ¼ cup of oil and heat until clams open.
2. Remove clams from shells and reserve.
3. Strain remaining oil and clam juice stock and reserve.
4. Sauté garlic in remaining half cup of oil until brown; then discard garlic.
5. Add tomatoes, salt and pepper, and cook until thickened.
6. Add reserved stock and clams and simmer until warm. Add parsley, more fresh pepper, and pour over spaghetti.

## SPAGHETTI CARBONARA
## FOR MORT SHUMAN

serves 4–6

1 clove garlic, sliced thin
3 slices bacon, cut into thin strips
4 tablespoons olive oil
2 tablespoons butter
½ cup prosciutto, sliced into thin strips
4 tablespoons grated Parmesan cheese
2 eggs, beaten
1 pound spaghetti, cooked *al dente*

1. Brown garlic and bacon gently in a frying pan. Pour off fat and remove garlic.
2. Add oil, butter and prosciutto. Sauté gently for 5 minutes but do not brown.
3. Remove from stove, stir in cheese and add eggs quickly.
4. Pour over spaghetti and toss well.

## LOVE FOR THE BLACK OLIVE

serves 4–6

*A lovely sauce with macaroni*

1 clove garlic, minced
½ teaspoon dried basil
oil
2 tomatoes, peeled and sliced in strips
1 pound spiral macaroni
2 tablespoons melted butter
½ cup grated Parmesan cheese
2 8-ounce packages mozzarella cheese, cubed
1 dozen pitted black olives, chopped coarsely
pepper to taste
2 teaspoons ground dried oregano

1. Sauté the garlic and basil in oil until garlic is golden; add the tomatoes.
2. Meanwhile, cook the macaroni until it is *al dente.* Drain and place in a warm dish.
3. Add to the macaroni melted butter, cheeses, olives and pepper. Add garlic and basil sauce, sprinkle with oregano, toss well and serve hot.

# COLD LO MEIN NOODLES

serves 4

 1 pound lo mein or thin whole wheat
    noodles
¼ cup sesame oil
½ cup tamari (soy sauce)
 4 scallions, chopped fine
 4 cloves garlic, crushed
 1 tablespoon grated ginger
dash of Tabasco (optional)
 2 tablespoons tahini (sesame paste)

1. Boil noodles until *al dente;* rinse well in
   cold water.
2. Heat sesame oil and toss noodles in it
   until thoroughly coated; then add tahini
   and toss well. Remove from pan and allow
   to cool.
3. Combine other ingredients and toss well
   with noodles. Refrigerate. Serve cold.

## TOMATO, BASIL AND PARSLEY SAUCE FOR METAPHYSICAL MORANDI

serves 4–6

1¼ pounds tomatoes, peeled and cut into
     strips
  6 fresh basil leaves
  1 bunch parsley, chopped (Italian parsley
     is preferred)
  salt and pepper to taste
  2 cloves garlic, sliced
  ½ cup olive oil
  1 pound linguine, cooked *al dente*
  1 cup grated Parmesan cheese

1. In a colander, drain tomatoes. Add basil, parsley, salt and pepper.
2. Meanwhile, heat garlic in oil until browned and then discard garlic.
3. Add tomatoes, basil, parsley and seasonings and sauté, being careful that tomatoes do not become mushy.
4. Pour sauce over linguine and toss well. Sprinkle with cheese.
5. Serve hot on pre-warmed plates.

## QUICK GARLIC AND OLIVE OIL WITH SPAGHETTI

serves 4–6

*This is as delicious as it is quick.*

   3 cloves garlic, crushed
¼ cup olive oil
   1 pound spaghetti, cooked *al dente*
   handful of chopped parsley
   freshly ground pepper to taste

1. Sauté garlic in oil until golden brown.
2. Pour over cooked spaghetti; sprinkle with parsley and pepper.

# THE VEGETARIAN'S SPAGHETTI

serves 4–6

 3 cloves garlic, crushed
 1 onion, chopped fine
½ cup olive oil
 6 tablespoons butter
 1 package frozen artichoke hearts, defrosted
½ pound mushrooms, sliced
½ pound fresh lima beans, parboiled
 2 green peppers, sliced into thin strips
 1 pound green peas
½ cup dry red wine
 4 medium tomatoes
salt and pepper to taste
 1 pound spaghetti, cooked *al dente*
grated Parmesan cheese

1. In a large pan, sauté garlic and onion in oil and butter until golden brown.
2. Add artichokes, mushrooms, beans, peppers, peas and red wine.
3. When the wine begins to simmer, add tomatoes and season with salt and pepper.
4. Cover and simmer over low heat until sauce is thickened.
5. Prepare a hot serving dish. Place cooked spaghetti in it and pour sauce over. Sprinkle with cheese.

# DIETER'S DELICIOUS PASTA

serves: 4

1 pound artichoke flour or whole wheat semolina
1 tablespoon olive oil
6 sun-dried tomatoes, soaked until soft in hot
   water then chopped
¼ pound mushrooms chopped
2 garlic cloves, crushed
   salt and pepper to taste
   crumbled tofu (optional)

1. Cook pasta until "al dente"; then strain.
2. Saute garlic until golden, add tomatoes and mushrooms and continue sauteeing until tender. Add seasonings and heat through.
3. Crumble tofu and sprinkle on top.

# LOW-CALORIE PESTO PRIMA

serves: 4

1 pound pasta (spiral macaroni is especially
　　nice for this)
½ pound soft tofu
4 garlic cloves, cut in quarters
3 tablespoons chopped fresh basil
3 tablespoons umeboshi paste*
　　fresh ground black pepper to taste


1. Cook pasta until "al dente." Rinse well and
   cool.
2. Blend remaining ingredients until mixture is
   smooth.
3. Spoon mixture on chilled pasta and mix well.
   This can be served on a bed of lettuce, garnished with radishes or tomatoes.

*Umeboshi paste is made from Oriental pickled plums avail-
able in natural food stores or you can substitute lemon juice
(1 whole lemon) and salt; but the umeboshi has a very distinct
exotic flavor.

**66** . . . O, he is as tedious
As a tired horse, a railing wife;
Worse than a smoky house. I had rather live
With cheese and garlic in a windmill far
Than feed on cates and have him talk to me
In any summer house in Christendom. **99**

SHAKESPEARE, *Henry IV, Part 1*

# Soups

# PEPE'S GARLIC SOUP BAKED IN THE OVEN

serves 4

French bread, stale and cut into thin slices
4 cups boiling salted water
8 cloves garlic
1 onion, chopped fine
1 teaspoon chopped parsley
2 tablespoons olive oil
1 teaspoon paprika
4 eggs

1. Preheat oven to 450°.
2. Place bread slices in a shallow heavy pot, and cover with boiling water. Cover pot and simmer until garlic mixture is ready.
3. Fry garlic, onion and parsley in oil until lightly browned. Remove garlic, add paprika and turn heat off immediately to prevent burning.
4. Add mixture to bread and water and place in oven without cover for about 15 minutes, or until crust forms on bread (place under broiler for a few minutes if necessary).
5. Place in bowls and break an egg into each bowl while soup is very hot.

## SOUPE À L'AIL (FRENCH GARLIC SOUP)

serves 8

24 cloves garlic, peeled but not cut
 2 tablespoons oil or drippings
 8 cups boiling water or stock
 pinch each of nutmeg, tarragon and ground
   cloves
 salt and pepper to taste
 4 egg yolks, beaten

1. In a large, heavy soup pot, lightly sauté garlic cloves in oil until they are golden.
2. Add boiling water or stock and seasonings and simmer slowly for about 20 minutes.
3. Allow to cool slightly, then put in a blender or through a food mill.
4. Heat slightly and add egg yolks gradually, stirring continuously. Do not allow soup to boil. Serve immediately, poured over toasted French bread.

## SUPER SOUP

serves 8–10

> 2 cups assorted beans (azuki, soy, kidney, lima, etc.)
> 2 onions, chopped
> 4 to 6 cloves garlic, chopped
> 1 bay leaf
> salt and pepper to taste
> 8 to 10 cups water
> 1 cup brown rice
> 1 cup assorted grains (kasha, bulgur, millet)
> 1 pound mixed vegetables
> ½ cup red lentils
> ½ cup sunflower seeds
> ½ cup walnuts
> dash of tamari (soy sauce)

1. Cook beans, onions, garlic, bay leaf and seasoning in water until beans are tender —about 2½ hours.
2. Add rice; after 20 minutes, add other grains.
3. Cook for another 20 minutes, then add mixed vegetables.
4. Add remaining ingredients, except tamari sauce, 2 minutes before serving.
5. Serve immediately with tamari sauce.

NOTE

If a thinner soup is desired, add more boiling water and adjust seasoning.

# PRIEST'S SOUP

serves 6

*This Spanish soup is so-called because of the addition of eggs: supposedly, priests lived well!*

1 onion, sliced
3 cloves garlic, sliced
2 tablespoons olive oil
2 tomatoes, sliced
1 bay leaf
5 cups boiling water
salt and pepper to taste
pinch of paprika
6 or 7 bread slices, cut into squares
6 or 7 eggs

1. Brown onion and garlic in oil.
2. Add tomatoes and bay leaf and sauté for 5 minutes.
3. Add water, cover and simmer for 15 to 20 minutes. Preheat oven to 350°
4. Add seasonings. In an ovenproof soup tureen or casserole, place bread, break eggs carefully and pour soup gently over eggs.
5. Bake until crust forms on top of soup; serve immediately.

## GARLIC GET-WELL BROTH

serves 1

   1 onion, chopped
   3 or 4 cloves garlic, peeled but not cut
  ½ teaspoon grated ginger
  ½ cup water
   mixed herbs such as parsley, thyme,
      rosemary
   salt and pepper to taste

Boil all ingredients until onions and garlic
are soft. Strain and serve hot.

## GARCIA'S GARLIC SOUP

serves 8

*You can cook a dish with a whole bulb, or more, of garlic, and far from being overwhelmed, create a delicate flavor provided that the garlic is not cut, but only peeled.*

1 bulb garlic
1 tablespoon butter
8 cups boiling water
salt and pepper to taste
½ cup chopped parsley
whole-grain bread slices

1. Separate cloves of garlic, peel but do not cut.
2. In a large heavy pan, sauté cloves in butter until golden brown.
3. Add water, salt and pepper and parsley, and simmer for 10 minutes.
4. Place 1 slice of bread on bottom of each bowl and pour soup over it. Serve very hot.

## YOGURT AND BARLEY SOUP TOUCHED BY A LEMON

serves 6

1 onion, chopped fine
1 clove garlic, chopped fine
1 tablespoon butter
6 cups clear soup stock
¾ cup pearl barley, soaked 6 to 8 hours
2 cups yogurt
juice of 1 lemon
salt and pepper to taste
1 tablespoon fresh mint or crushed dried
    mint

1. Sauté onion and garlic in butter until golden.
2. Add soup stock and bring to a boil.
3. Add barley, cover and simmer over low heat for 1 hour.
4. Combine yogurt and lemon juice with a small amount of soup.
5. Remove soup from heat and very gradually add yogurt mixture.
6. Heat, if necessary, before serving, but be careful not to bring to boil or soup will curdle.
7. Serve garnished with mint.

NOTE

This soup is also delicious when chilled.

## GROWING TIPS

Garlic has not been grown from seed for thousands of years, but it is not difficult to grow. Plant outer cloves of good size, 2 inches deep and 6 inches apart. Indoors, garlic cloves can be planted 6 to a 10-inch pot. A rich, light, well-drained soil and a climate where the growing season is long and the daytime temperature high is best (garlic grown in cold or damp areas tends to be inferior). Garlic is usually harvested 6 to 8 months after planting: "Plant on the longest and reap on the shortest day."

The Romans claimed that garlic planted during a full moon would be round like an onion (not divided into cloves) and milder.

When drying garlic, braid the green tops together and hang in ropes in a dry place. Europeans buy it this way (and use it quickly!), and it's most decorative hanging in the kitchen.

Growing garlic in a clay pot

# Vegetable dishes

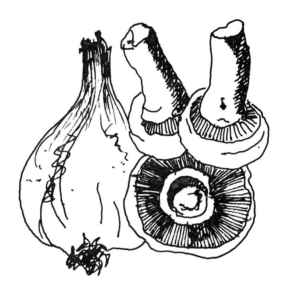

Cultivating garlic, 15th century woodcut

# PANDIT PRANATH'S CURRY

serves 8

*This curry is so authentic that at least one of the ingredients (oregano seed) can be purchased only at a store specializing in Indian products.*

 2 tablespoons coriander seed
 1 tablespoon cumin seed
 1 teaspoon oregano seed
 4 onions, chopped fine
 4 cloves garlic, chopped fine
 2 inches ginger root, grated
 3 fresh hot green chilis, diced
 ¼ pound clarified butter (ghee)
 ¾ teaspoon turmeric
 ¾ teaspoon cayenne pepper
 ¾ teaspoon salt

1. Grind seeds in an electric grinder or with mortar and pestle.
2. Brown onions, garlic, ginger, seeds and chilis very slowly in ghee. Add seasonings. Keep mixture liquid; add water or chopped tomatoes if necessary.

NOTE

This curry can be mixed with a wide variety of vegetables and is especially delicious cooked with beets, dried beans or chopped spinach.

# SOYBEANS THAT DEFY DETECTION

*Don't tell anyone what this is until after they've eaten it. Soak the soybeans as long as you can without sprouting them; the longer you soak them, the quicker the cooking and the more digestible the eating.*

1 cup soybeans, soaked at least 8 hours
6 cloves garlic, minced fine
1 onion, chopped fine
2 tablespoons oil
salt and pepper to taste
pinch of ginger powder or grated fresh ginger
1 tablespoon miso (soybean paste)
2 or more tablespoons molasses

1. In the water in which they soaked, cook the soybeans until tender.
2. Sauté garlic and onion in oil until golden; add seasonings.
3. Dilute miso with enough cold water to make a smooth, creamy consistency and combine with molasses.
4. Combine all ingredients and simmer slowly on top of stove for about 10 minutes or bake in a slow oven (300°) for about 15 minutes.

## EASY GARLIC PICKLES

yield: 2 jars

20 small cucumbers
 2 quarts water
½ cup white vinegar
 8 tablespoons coarse salt or 10 tablespoons
      sea salt
 1 teaspoon mustard seed
 1 teaspoon turmeric
 6 cloves garlic
 2 bay leaves
 2 hot chili peppers (optional)
 fresh dill

1. Scrub cucumbers well and fit tightly into
   jars.
2. Boil water, vinegar, salt, mustard and
   turmeric.
3. Allow liquid to cool and pour equally into
   each jar of cucumbers.
4. Top jars with garlic cloves, 1 bay leaf,
   some chili pepper and fresh dill.
5. Seal jars well and keep in a warm place,
   being careful to keep cucumbers covered
   with the liquid (add additional water if
   necessary).

NOTE

Pickles are ready to eat in a few days—when
the cucumbers turn yellow. After this, keep
them in the refrigerator and use soon; they
will not last more than a few weeks.

## PAUL PRICE'S PRICELESS ENCHILLADAS

serves 8–10

*Be prepared to spend the whole day making this dish—it's worth it!*

STOCK

4 onions, chopped
2 yellow squash, chopped
4 stalks celery, chopped
2 green peppers, chopped
2 carrots, chopped
2 quarts water

SAUCE

½ cup vegetable or peanut oil
8 tablespoons flour
4 tablespoons chili powder
6 cloves garlic, crushed
salt and pepper to taste
½ teaspoon cumin powder
½ teaspoon coriander powder
½ teaspoon basil
½ teaspoon marjoram
½ teaspoon cinnamon
2 dried hot peppers, crushed
½ tablespoon tahini (sesame paste)
1 tablespoon peanut butter
1 tablespoon carob powder

## LAYERS

36 tortillas
10 onions, chopped fine
 1 pound spinach, steamed
 1 pound snow peas (optional)
 1 pound mushrooms
 2 ripe avocados, sliced*
 1 grapefruit, sliced*
 1 pint sour cream or yogurt
 hot green chilis (optional)
 1 can black olives, sliced
 3 pounds Monterey Jack cheese, sliced

1. Boil vegetables in water until slightly firm; then strain and discard and use liquid for stock.
2. Make a roux by heating oil, adding flour and stirring until brown. Add chili powder, then stock, stirring continuously.
3. Add remaining sauce ingredients and simmer over low heat, stirring occasionally, for at least 4 hours.
4. Preheat oven to 350°.
5. Fry tortillas quickly on each side in deep hot oil; then dip lightly in sauce.
6. In a large casserole, layer ingredients as follows: tortillas, vegetables, sour cream or yogurt, chilis, olives, cheese and sauce. Finish with a layer of sauce and cheese.
7. Bake for a half hour. Serve with refried beans.

*Do not use if dish is to be reheated.

# DRIED BEANS WITH GARLIC SAUCE

serves 4

*Here is another example of a lot of garlic used as a mild flavoring.*

  1 pound white or black beans, soaked 6
     hours
  1 bulb of garlic, peeled but not cut
½ cup olive oil
  1 clove garlic, minced
  1 teaspoon cumin seed, crushed or
     powdered
  1 tablespoon salt

1. Place beans and garlic bulb in a large pot
   and cover with the water in which the
   beans had been soaking; cook until beans
   are almost tender—about an hour.
2. Drain water, remove garlic and place
   beans in a bean pot.
3. In a small skillet, heat oil and sauté minced
   clove until golden. Remove garlic and add
   cumin and salt to oil.
4. Add oil mixture to beans and cook,
   uncovered, for about 25 minutes, or until
   beans are completely cooked.

# MARCIA'S MARVELOUS RATATOUILLE

serves 4

4 or more cloves garlic, chopped fine
olive oil for sautéing
1 medium eggplant, cut in 1-inch cubes
3 zucchini, cut in 1-inch cubes
2 green peppers, sliced
1 onion, sliced
3 tomatoes, cut in chunks
1 teaspoon crushed oregano
1 bay leaf
salt and pepper to taste
Parmesan cheese (optional)

1. Preheat oven to 300°.
2. Sauté garlic in oil until golden, remove garlic and set aside.
3. Sauté eggplant and zucchini quickly until lightly browned and remove to ovenproof casserole.
4. Add more oil and garlic, if necessary, and sauté peppers, onion, tomatoes, oregano and bay leaf until onion is golden. When finished sautéing, add reserved garlic cloves, salt and pepper.
5. Layer in a deep casserole, eggplant and zucchini, cheese (if used), onion and tomatoes and bake for 1 hour. Remove bay leaf before serving.

## NOTE

*Ratatouille* is excellent served cold as an antipasto. There is an added advantage: it can be easily converted to a top-of-the-stove dish; omit the cheese, mix all the vegetables together (after initial sautéing), cover and simmer over low heat for about 20 minutes.

# ANDIE'S MIXED PICKLED VEGETABLES

   1 cup olive oil
1½ cups vinegar
   4 cloves garlic, crushed
   salt and pepper to taste
  ⅓ cup sugar
   cauliflower, broken into flowerets
   turnips, sliced thick
   green peppers, sliced thick
   asparagus, bottom of stalks removed and
      cut in half
   mushrooms, sliced or caps only
   small white onions
   Greek olives (the more shrivelled, the
      better)

1. Boil oil, vinegar, garlic, salt, pepper and sugar.
2. Allow to cook for about 5 minutes and pour over vegetables.
3. Cover and refrigerate for at least 24 hours; when serving, restore vegetables to room temperature so that dressing will liquify.

NOTE

This dish will last for a long time if properly covered and refrigerated.

# PEAS SAVANAROLA

serves 4

1 clove garlic, crushed
¼ cup olive oil
1 pound fresh green peas, shelled or 1
    package frozen peas, thawed
½ cup ham, diced
2 tablespoons minced parsley
½ cup water
1 teaspoon salt
¼ teaspoon white pepper

1. Combine all ingredients (except salt and pepper) in a pan and bring to a boil.
2. Cover and cook over low heat for 15 minutes.
3. Season to taste and serve hot.

# WINONA CATO'S POTATOES WITH GARLIC

serves 6–8

2½ pounds potatoes, peeled and quartered
30 to 40 cloves garlic, unpeeled
boiling water
½ cup butter
2 tablespoons flour
1 cup light cream or milk
heavy cream
salt and pepper to taste
fresh dill or parsley, chopped

1. Cook potatoes until soft enough to put through food mill or ricer.
2. Meanwhile, place garlic in pan, cover with boiling water and simmer for 1 minute; drain.
3. Heat one-half of butter in pan, peel garlic and sauté in butter over low heat until tender. Do not allow garlic to brown.
4. Add flour and stir until well blended; add light cream and stir continuously until mixture is smooth.
5. Remove from heat and puree mixture in food mill or blender; keep warm.
6. Combine riced potatoes and garlic sauce; add heavy cream and mix until desired consistency is obtained. Add seasoning and garnish with dill or parsley. Serve hot.

## SINFULLY SIMPLE GARLIC-FLAVORED POTATO CHIPS

Put potato chips in a container. Peel a clove or two of garlic and place it with the chips for a few hours. Remove the garlic, crisp the chips (if necessary) and wow your guests.

## A REAL INDIAN DAL

serves 3–4

3 cups water
1 cup red lentils, rinsed well and drained
1 clove garlic, chopped fine
2 tablespoons ghee (clarified butter) or
    vegetable oil
1 teaspoon salt
pinch cayenne pepper

1. Boil water and cook lentils over low heat for about 20 minutes, or until soft.
2. Meanwhile, sauté garlic in ghee or oil until golden.
3. Combine garlic, salt and pepper; add mixture to lentils, mixing well.
4. Serve hot with rice and yogurt on the side.

# GARLIC-ONION STEW

serves 4–6

8 onions, sliced thick
8 cloves garlic, minced
6 tablespoons oil
4 teaspoons flour
2 teaspoons paprika
salt to taste
1 bay leaf
vinegar to taste
dash of Worcestershire sauce
water

1. Sauté onions and garlic in 5 tablespoons oil until golden.
2. In a separate pan, make a gravy of remaining oil, flour, paprika and salt and cook until thick.
3. Add gravy to onion-garlic mixture; add bay leaf, vinegar, Worcestershire sauce and enough water to cover.
4. Cover and simmer over low heat until onions are soft. Serve hot.

## STEAMED KALE

serves **8**

  2 pounds kale
  4 cloves garlic, crushed
  3 tablespoons olive oil
  ½ cup water
  ½ teaspoon salt

1. Wash kale well and shake, leaving some water remaining.
2. Sauté garlic in olive oil until golden, add water and salt, and bring to a boil.
3. Add kale, lower heat, cover and cook for 6 to 8 minutes, or until tender.
4. Remove from pan and chop kale with two sharp knives or a chopper until vegetable is coarsely shredded. Serve immediately.

# THE NEW JERUSALEM ARTICHOKES

serves 4

4 cloves garlic, sliced fine
2 tablespoons butter or oil
1 pound Jerusalem artichokes
water or vegetable broth (optional)

1. Sauté garlic in butter or oil until golden.
2. Meanwhile, scrub Jerusalem artichokes
   well and cut horizontally in ¼-inch slices.
3. Add Jerusalem artichokes to pan, cover
   and simmer over low heat until tender, yet
   crisp. Check after 5 minutes to see if more
   liquid is necessary, and if so, add a small
   amount of water or broth. Serve warm.

# HUNGARIAN BROWN BAKE

serves 2

1 pound potatoes, peeled and sliced very
    thin
2 cloves garlic, crushed
salt and pepper to taste
pinch grated nutmeg
1 egg
1 cup milk
1 cup grated Cheddar cheese
breadcrumbs
butter

1. Preheat oven to 350°.
2. Soak potatoes in cold water.
3. Butter a casserole and rub it with the garlic.
4. Drain potatoes and place in casserole with
   seasonings.
5. Beat egg, milk and one half of cheese
   together and pour over potatoes.
6. Add remaining cheese, lightly sprinkle with
   breadcrumbs and dot with liberal amount of
   butter.
7. Bake until potatoes are cooked and top is
   dark gold.

# MARILYN'S MILLET

serves 3–4

1 onion, sliced fine
2 stalks celery, chopped
1 green pepper, sliced
2 carrots, sliced fine
2 zucchini, ½-inch thick slices
1 tomato, chopped
2 tablespoons vegetable or peanut oil
1 cup millet (couscous may be substituted)
2 cups boiling broth
1 teaspoon curry powder
3 garlic cloves, crushed
½ teaspoon ginger powder
salt and pepper to taste

1. Sauté vegetables briefly (no more than 7 minutes) in oil; drain and set aside.
2. If any more than a coating of oil remains on skillet, wipe it off. Brown millet, stirring continuously so it does not burn.
3. Add broth, vegetables and remaining ingredients, cover tightly and simmer over low heat until millet is cooked.

## NOTE

Cubed chicken or shrimp may be added to this dish.

# SPANISH NUTTY RICE

serves 4–6

  2 large Spanish onions, sliced thin
  2 cloves garlic, minced
  2 tablespoons oil
  2 cups rice
½ pound mixed nuts, chopped
  4 cups boiling water
  2 sweet green or red peppers, sliced
  2 teaspoons saffron
  2 tablespoons parsley, chopped

1. Sauté onions and garlic in oil until brown.
2. Add rice and nuts; stir well and cook
   until all oil is absorbed.
3. Add water, bring to boiling point, cover and
   cook over low heat until all liquid has been
   absorbed.
4. Meanwhile, sauté peppers.
5. Remove rice from pan, add saffron,
   parsley and peppers. Serve hot.

# Egg dishes

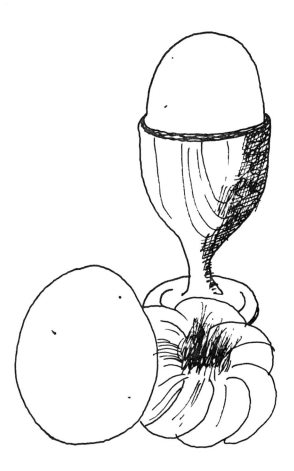

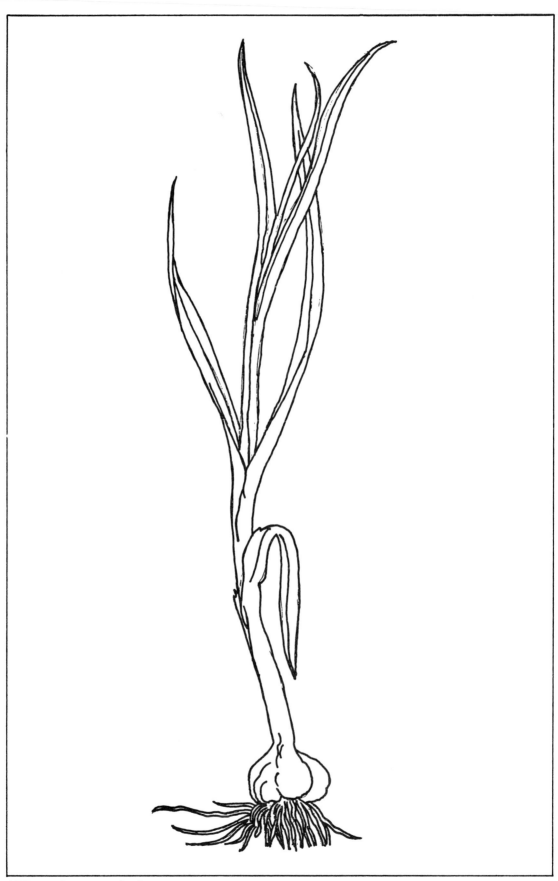

15th century woodcut

## BE-DEVILLED EGGS

½ teaspoon ground or grated ginger
2 cloves garlic, crushed
½ cup dark rum
6 hard-boiled egg yolks

1. Combine the first 3 ingredients and marinate egg yolks in the mixture for at least 6 hours.
2. Remove yolks from marinade, mash or cut in half and serve cold on toast or crackers with mayonnaise or *béarnais* sauce.

## SYRIAN THETCHOUKA

serves 6

4 onions, sliced
4 tablespoons olive oil
3 cloves garlic, minced
4 sweet green or red peppers, sliced
6 tomatoes, sliced
salt and pepper to taste
6 eggs
½ cup sharp cheese, grated fine

1. Preheat oven to 350°.
2. Sauté onions in oil until golden.
3. Add garlic, vegetables and seasoning, cover and cook over low heat until vegetables are tender.
4. Butter a large casserole and transfer mixture into it. Make 6 hollows in mixture and carefully drop an egg into each hollow. Sprinkle with grated cheese and cover.
5. Bake for 10 minutes, or until eggs are set.

## EGGS A LOT DIFFERENT THAN BENEDICT

serves 6

1 orange, cut in half
1 bulb garlic, unpeeled
salt to taste
½ teaspoon minced fresh or dried hot
      pepper
12 asparagus tips, cooked
6 egg yolks
½ pound mild cheese (not Cheddar) cut in
      thin slices
6 English muffins

1. Preheat oven to 325°.
2. Crush orange—pulp and skin—in the
   bottom of a greased pan, remove orange
   making sure the oil from the skin remains
   on the pan.
3. Crush garlic into pan, add salt and hot
   pepper, mix well.
4. The less hearty may remove the garlic at
   this point. Add asparagus tips, egg yolks
   and cheese. Bake until cheese melts.
5. Serve on toasted English muffins, on which
   some orange has been rubbed.

## BETTINA'S BIRD NEST EGGS ON ESCAROLE

serves 3–4

    1 pound escarole
    water
    salt to taste
    2 tablespoons olive oil
    2 cloves garlic, minced
2½ tablespoons flour
1¼ cups milk
  ½ cup Parmesan cheese, freshly grated
    salt and pepper to taste
    3 or 4 poached eggs
    3 or 4 teaspoons butter

1. Wash escarole thoroughly and shred.
   Steam in small amount of water until
   tender; add salt.
2. Meanwhile, heat oil in a heavy pan, add
   garlic and sauté until golden.
3. Add flour and stir until smooth. Quickly,
   add milk and stir continuously until mixture
   thickens. Add one half of Parmesan
   cheese, salt and pepper.
4. Add one third of sauce to escarole; mix
   well and divide into three or four individual
   small baking casseroles.
5. Place 1 poached egg on top of each
   casserole and cover with remaining sauce.
   Top with remaining grated cheese and
   dot with butter.
6. Brown lightly under broiler and serve
   immediately.

## THEY'RE AGAINST IT, REGARDLESS...

"It has a vehement heat, and hot things send up vapors to the brain."

In earlier days when people spoke of "humors" and certain foods were prohibited to certain personality types, garlic was *verboten* for the ill-tempered, supposedly because it would add fuel to the fire. It could, however, be eaten with impunity by the mild-mannered.

Mohammed said that when Satan left the Garden of Eden garlic grew where he had stepped with his left foot, and onion his right. "Let none approach our mosques who eats garlic, onions, or leeks." In the *Hadith* of Mohammed, disobedience amounted to no more than a minor sin and went unpunished, but because Friday is mosque day, there used to be an edict against eating garlic on Friday.

According to one seventeenth-century writer, the English puritans believed that men who ate great quantities of garlic and onions and who fasted inordinately or studied too hard, had children subject to madness and/or melancholia.

Although ancient Egypt was the largest producer and probably the largest consumer of garlic, the priests considered it so unclean that anyone having eaten it could not enter the sacred temple of Cybele, the earth goddess.

The Japanese are one of the few peoples who do not generally use garlic in cooking. The reason most often given is that the pungency is just too overpowering for the delicate and clear taste of Japanese food. But garlic does have a place in the oriental medicine chest: garlic is used in "moxabustion," a form of acupuncture using heat instead of needles. A thin slice of garlic is placed on the skin over a pressure point, a small piece (about the size of a half grain of rice) of "moxa" (mugwort) is placed over this and lit with a piece of incense. The substance burns very slowly giving off an even heat. The garlic prevents scarring.

A fourteenth-century king of Castile made it a condition for his garlic-eating knights not to be able to appear before him for at least a month after their indulgence.

Imagine the ostracism of garlic in eighteenth-century England! This reference from a letter written by Shelley is probably typical: "What do you think? Young women of rank actually eat—you will never guess what—*garlick!* Our poor friend Lord Byron is quite corrupted by living among these people [Italians—ed.] and in fact, is going on in a way not worthy of him."

# Fish dishes

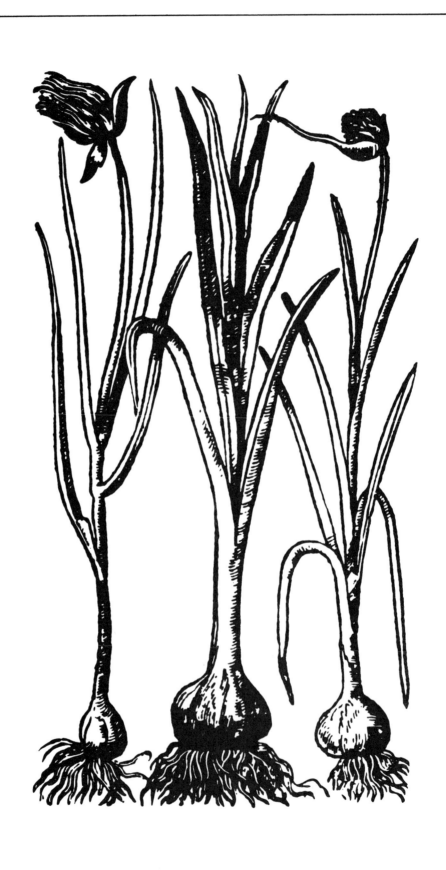

16th century woodcut

# TINA'S TUNA STEAK

serves 6

½ cup olive oil
1 bay leaf
salt and pepper to taste
½ onion, chopped
2 tuna steaks (about 1¼ pounds each)
oil
2 cloves garlic, chopped
1 tablespoon chopped parsley
2 tablespoons chopped capers

1. Combine olive oil, bay leaf, salt, pepper
   and onion, and marinate tuna steaks in
   mixture for about 1 hour.
2. Preheat oven for about 10 minutes. Remove
   tuna from marinade and place on broiling
   rack.
3. Broil until both sides are brown and then
   reduce heat; broil for an additional
   5 minutes on each side, basting
   occasionally with marinade.
4. When fish is done, season with a mixture
   of oil, garlic, parsley and capers and serve
   at once.

# FISHERMAN-STYLE CLAMS

serves 4

*This is a great dish to cook on the beach.*

24 cherrystone clams, washed and scrubbed
    well
 1 bunch of parsley, chopped
 4 cloves garlic, chopped fine

1. Put clams in a heavy, covered skillet over
   high flame.
2. When shells start to open, add parsley and
   garlic, remove lid and cook until clams are
   tender (usually when they are fully
   opened).
3. Serve with the cooking liquid.

# AN EASY ALMOST-BOUILLABAISSE

serves 6

*This is more of a stew than a soup—but with more water you can turn it into the latter.*

3 sweet green or red peppers, chopped
2 onions, chopped
5 cloves garlic, crushed
4 tablespoons olive oil
handful of parsley, chopped fine
2 pounds each of bass and whiting, cut in
    thick slices
water
¾ cup dry white wine
salt and pepper to taste
mussels in their shells (optional)
flour

1. Sauté peppers, onions and garlic in olive oil until golden; add parsley and simmer slowly for about 2 minutes.
2. Add fish and enough water to barely cover; boil over fairly high heat, covered, for about 15 minutes.
3. Add wine, seasoning and mussels (if used); cover and cook for about 3 minutes. Remove cover, stir in enough flour to thicken slightly and cook for an additional 5 minutes.

# THE BLACK CAT'S SHRIMP

serves 4

  6 cloves garlic, crushed
  1 teaspoon red pepper, crushed
  1 cup lemon juice
  1 cup olive oil
  3 teaspoons parsley, chopped
24 large shrimp, shelled and deveined

1. Mix all ingredients except shrimp.
2. Pour mixture over shrimp and marinate for at least 8 hours in refrigerator.
3. Remove from marinade and broil for 5 minutes on each side; baste with marinade.
4. Serve hot.

# PABLO'S ESCARGOTS

serves 2

½ pound butter
1 tablespoon lemon juice
1 teaspoon each garlic and shallot, chopped
    fine
1 teaspoon Worcestershire sauce
pinch each ground thyme and rosemary
12 snails, cooked

1. Cream butter and beat in lemon juice
   gradually.
2. Add garlic, shallot, seasonings, and herbs.
3. Mix with snails and replace in shells; chill
   until ready to serve.

# YANGTSE GARLICKED CRAB

serves 4

1 cup chicken stock
1 cup sweet sauterne or Chinese wine
1 teaspoon cornstarch
1 teaspoon salt
2 teaspoons fresh ginger, chopped
2 teaspoons sugar
4 scallions, cut in 1-inch lengths
1 pound cracked crab
4 cloves garlic, crushed

1. Heat chicken stock and wine in a large frying pan.
2. Add cornstarch, salt, ginger, sugar and scallions. Cook slowly until scallions are done, but still firm.
3. Add crab and cook for 5 minutes; add garlic, stir and cook for a few more minutes.
4. Serve immediately with rice.

# GARLIC AND CURRIED SHRIMP

serves 6

1½ pounds shrimp
  2 teaspoons turmeric powder
  ¼ cup vegetable oil
  2 cloves garlic, chopped
  2 onions, sliced
  1 green pepper, chopped
  1 teaspoon powdered cardamon
1½ teaspoons salt
  2 teaspoons fresh ginger, chopped

1. Wash shrimp and sprinkle with turmeric.
2. Steam in a pan without water for 2 to 3 minutes until shrimp are pink. Remove from pan; shell and devein.
3. Brown shrimp in oil. Add the rest of the ingredients and cook slowly, stirring until most of liquid evaporates.
4. Serve hot over rice.

## BAKED "KNOBL" CARP

serves 4–6

  6 cloves garlic, crushed
  2 teaspoons salt
½ teaspoon pepper
  1 tablespoon paprika
  3 tablespoons vegetable oil
  1 carp, sliced

1. Preheat oven to 325°.
2. Combine garlic, seasonings and oil, and blend into a smooth paste; rub well into carp slices.
3. Oil baking dish and place fish in it.
4. Bake, turning frequently, for about 1 hour, or until fish is very dried and brown.
5. Allow to cool and then refrigerate. Serve cold.

## THE DRUNKEN FISHERMAN'S RICE AND SHRIMP

serves 6

1¼ pounds shrimp, shelled and deveined
  2 cloves garlic, chopped
 ¼ of an onion, chopped
 ¼ cup olive oil
   salt and pepper to taste
  1 cup dry white wine
 ¼ cup brandy
  4 tablespoons butter
  2 cups rice
  1 quart clam juice, heated
  2 tablespoons olive oil

1. Rinse shrimp well.
2. Sauté garlic and onion in ¼ cup olive oil until golden brown.
3. Add shrimp and cook slowly over low heat. Season with salt and pepper; add wine and brandy and simmer for about 8 to 10 minutes; keep warm.
4. In another pan, melt butter and add rice. Stir continuously until all butter is absorbed and rice becomes somewhat dry.
5. Add a small amount of the shrimp sauce and a small amount of clam juice and allow rice to absorb liquids. Continue the process, allowing enough time for absorption, until all sauce and juice is used up. Cover and cook over low heat until rice is cooked.
6. Add the 2 tablespoons of olive oil and place rice in a warm serving dish. Serve hot with the shrimp.

# SOLE FOR SIDNEY BECHET

serves 6

SAUCE

2 eggs
2 cloves garlic
2 slices bread
juice and grated rind of ½ a lemon
1 cup olive oil (the French "James Plagniol"
    is superb for this)
salt and pepper to taste

6 bay leaves
1 lemon, sliced thin
6 sole fillets
dry white wine

1. To make sauce: boil eggs and garlic cloves until eggs are hard boiled.
2. Trim crust off bread.
3. Combine lemon juice, rind, olive oil, salt and pepper. Pour slowly into food mill or blender together with bread, eggs and garlic and blend.
4. Keep sauce warm in a double boiler.
5. Place bay leaves and lemon slices on bottom of shallow pan. Place sole fillets on top and cover with wine.
6. Simmer over low heat for about 15 minutes; pour sauce over fillets and serve hot.

# WOKKED-OUT SWEET AND SOUR FISH

serves 4

1½ to 2 pounds striped bass
   2 tablespoons sesame or peanut oil
   2 cloves garlic, crushed
   1 teaspoon grated fresh ginger
   boiling water
   1 tablespoon Japanese rice wine or dry
      sherry
  ½ cup molasses or Chinese brown sauce
   1 teaspoon fruit jam or preserves
   1 tablespoon tamari (soy sauce)
  ⅓ cup vinegar
   2 tablespoons cornstarch

1. Slash fish along backbone crosswise on each side.
2. In a wok, heat oil and sauté garlic and ginger until slightly brown.
3. Place fish in wok and barely cover with boiling water and rice wine or sherry.
4. Lower heat, cover and cook for 5 minutes; then remove from wok and allow to stand about 15 minutes.
5. Meanwhile, combine other ingredients and cook in wok until thickened. Pour over fish while still hot.
6. Serve on rice.

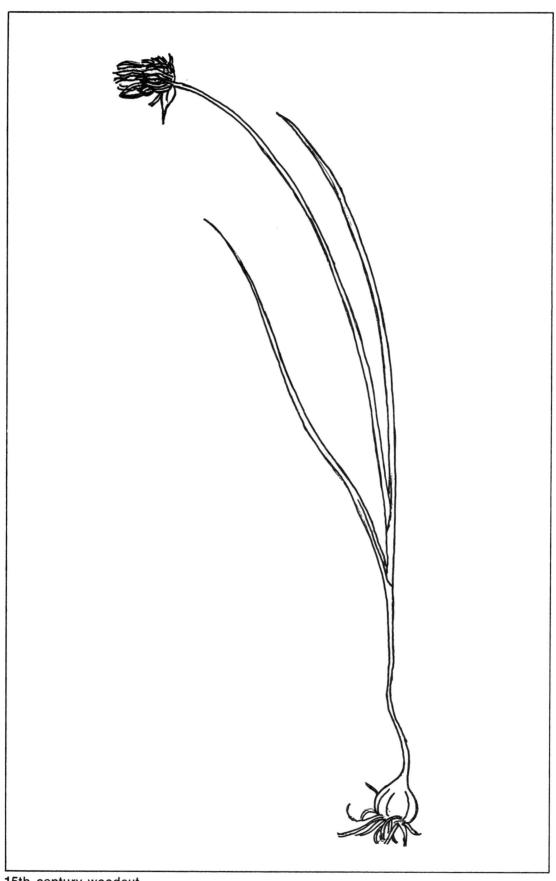

15th century woodcut

## "POOR MAN'S TREACLE" OR THE FOOD OF THE "LOWER" CLASSES

"Don't go near them! They've eaten garlic!"
Aristophanes

Aristophanes was following the "party line" of most high-born Greeks in his disdain of garlic. The Romans followed suit; garlic was food for the *hoi polloi,* not fit for gentlemen like Horace, who called it more poisonous than hemlock. A Frenchman once remarked upon reading Horace: *Horace, si tu l'avais gouté ... / Tu aurais mieux aimé ta tête couronnée / D'une chaine d'ail que de laurier.* Translated: "Horace, if you had tasted it ... / You had rather be crowned with garlic / Than with laurel."

Garlic was food for slaves; it was the daily ration for thousands who built the great pyramids. Herod supposedly spent the equivalent of two million dollars on garlic to feed the workers who rebuilt the temple in Jerusalem—this was hardly done to please their palates but more because of garlic's strength-building, sickness-preventing qualities.

When Marco Polo traveled through China in the thirteenth century, he noted that meat and poultry often was eaten raw. "The poorer sort go to the shambles and take the raw liver as soon as it is drawn from the beasts, then they chop it up small, put it in garlic sauce and eat it then and there."

# IN OTHER WORDS...

Old English—*Garleac*
Greek—*Skortho*
Latin—*Unio*—*Allium satiuum* (botanical)
Irish-Gaelic—*Gairleog*
German—*Knoblauch*
Portuguese—*Alho*
Japanese—*Ninniku*
Hawaiian—*Aka'akai*—*pilau, 'aka' akai—
    pupu, kalika*
Zulu—*Ishaladi len yoka; isweli lasendle*
Swahili—*Kitunguu sauma*
Finnish—*Valkosipuli*
Cornish—*Kenynen ewynek*
Yiddish—*Knobl*
Russian—*Chesnok*
Spanish—*Ajo*
French—*Ail*
Swedish—*Vitlok*
Arabic—*Thum*
Dutch—*Knoflook*
Italian—*Aglio*
Chinese—*Suan*
Hebrew—*Shum*

# Meat dishes

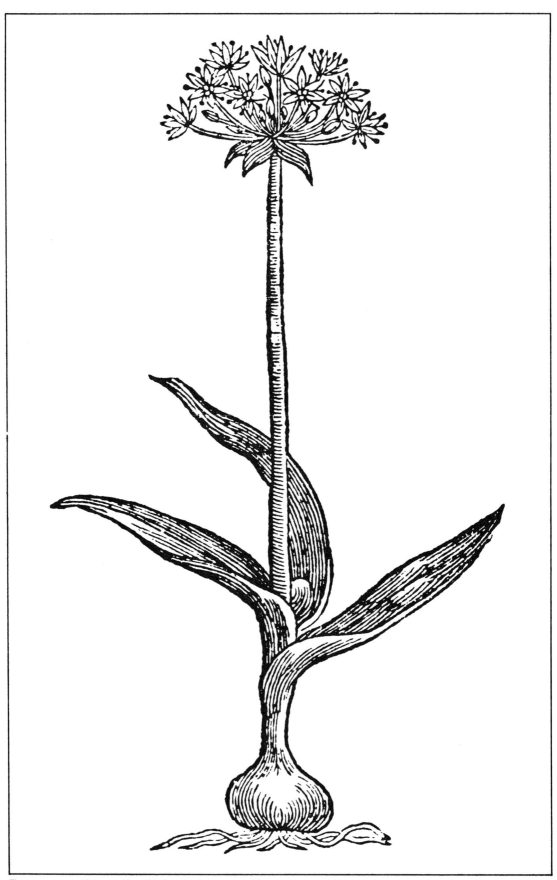

European wild garlic, 16th century woodcut

# TEXAS VIRGIL'S LEG OF LAMB

serves 4–6

    8 fresh rosemary leaves or ½ teaspoon
       dried rosemary
    1 3–4 pound leg of lamb
    4 cloves garlic, slivered
    2 teaspoons salt
   ½ teaspoon freshly ground pepper
    4 tablespoons butter
1½ cups dry white wine

1. Preheat oven to 450°.
2. If using dried rosemary, roll garlic in it.
3. Cut slits in leg of lamb and insert garlic. If using rosemary leaves, insert in slits with garlic.
4. Rub leg of lamb with salt and pepper.
5. Place in shallow roasting pan and dab with butter. Roast for 25 minutes, or until browned.
6. Pour off fat and add wine. Reduce heat to 350° and roast for another hour, or until tender. Baste frequently.

# MEAT ROLLS VIA ROUMANIA

serves 4–6

3 cloves garlic, crushed
2 pounds ground beef
1 onion, minced fine
3 eggs, lightly beaten
3 tablespoons water
2 teaspoons salt
pepper to taste
4 tablespoons flour
½ teaspoon paprika

1. Combine garlic, beef, onion, eggs, water, salt and pepper.
2. Shape into rolls approximately 3 inches long and 1 inch wide.
3. Combine flour and paprika and roll meat in mixture.
4. Brown slowly in hot oil until well cooked; or broil (without coating).

## THE CHILI-MAN'S DREAM

yield: 6 quarts

3 10-ounce cans chicken broth
3 pounds flank steak (all fat removed), cut
     into ⅜-inch cubes
5 pounds pork chops (all fat and bones
     removed), cut into ⅜-inch cubes
3 8-ounce cans stewed tomatoes
1 7-ounce can diced green chili peppers
4 cloves garlic, chopped fine
2 teaspoons oregano
2 teaspoons ground cumin
3 tablespoons chili powder
3 teaspoons black pepper
1 tablespoon brown sugar
1 cup chopped onions
1 cup chopped green pepper
1 pound Monterey Jack cheese
juice of 1 lime
salt to taste

1. Mix all ingredients up to (and including)
   brown sugar together in a large pan.
   Bring to a boil and simmer for 1 hour.
2. Add onions and green peppers and simmer
   another 4 hours.
3. Add cheese and stir well until the right
   consistency for chili.
4. Add lime juice and salt. Serve hot.

# PSHAR

serves 4

*By any name this dish of jellied calves feet is a delicacy.*

1 or 2 calves feet
2 onions, diced
4 or more cloves garlic
1 tablespoon or more salt (gelatin absorbs
    salt, so be generous)
pepper to taste
2 tablespoons vinegar
water to cover

1. Simmer all ingredients together for 3 hours, or until meat falls apart from bones; pour off water and reserve.
2. Place meat on platter and cover with a thin layer of liquid.
3. Allow to cool and then refrigerate (hard-boiled egg slices may be added).
4. When jelled, cut into cubes and serve as a side dish.

NOTE

Although not as traditional, pshar can be served hot as soup over garlic-flavored bread.

# PORTABELLO PORK TENDERLOIN

serves 6

  2 cloves garlic, crushed
  1 teaspoon rosemary
¼ teaspoon sage
    salt and pepper to taste
  3 pounds pork tenderloin
12 slices lean bacon
  5 tablespoons butter
  5 tablespoons olive oil
½ cup dry white wine

1. Preheat oven to 325°.
2. Combine garlic, herbs and seasonings.
3. Parboil pork for about 15 minutes.
4. Press garlic mixture into pork with the tip of a spoon.
5. Tie bacon around pork.
6. Heat butter and oil and brown pork on all sides.
7. Place pork in a casserole, pour wine over it, and bake for a half hour or until well cooked; turn and baste frequently.
8. When pork is cooked, remove bacon, place on platter, add water and seasonings to taste to remaining pan juices to make a gravy and serve at once.

# VENISON DOMINQUIN

serves 4

*This dish should be cooked quickly and the meat should be slightly rare for maximum enjoyment.*

½ cup olive oil
 4 cloves garlic, sliced thin
 salt and pepper to taste
 1 pound venison steak,* sliced in thin strips
     (at room temperature)
½ cup dry red wine

1. Heat oil in a large pan; add garlic and sauté over medium heat until garlic is golden. Add salt and pepper.
2. Add venison and turn continuously until meat starts to brown.
3. Add wine, heat and remove from fire immediately. Serve over rice.

*Beef can be substituted if venison is not available.

# THE BEER DRINKER'S CHICKEN

serves 6

3 cloves garlic, sliced thin
2 large onions, sliced
6 tablespoons butter
2 tablespoons oil
1 3½–4 pound chicken
¼ cup flour
salt and pepper to taste
2 cups beer
1 cup heavy cream

1. Preheat oven to 350°.
2. Sauté garlic and onions gently in butter and oil until golden; drain and set aside garlic and onions.
3. Sprinkle chicken with flour.
4. Sauté chicken in the butter and oil for 15 minutes, turning frequently to brown on all sides.
5. Place chicken in a casserole, sprinkle with salt and pepper and pour beer over it.
6. Bake for about 1¼ hours, or until cooked, occasionally basting with the beer sauce.
7. When chicken is done, put onion and garlic mixture in a blender and puree.
8. Pour puree over chicken, heat and then add cream.
9. As soon as cream is warm, serve with rice or garlic potatoes (see p. 88).

# SINIYA (ISRAELI)

serves 4

1 pound ground beef
salt and pepper to taste
¾ teaspoon ground cumin
¾ teaspoon ground coriander
1 teaspoon chopped mint
2 tablespoons pine nuts
dill
parsley
1 cup tahini (sesame paste)
2 cloves garlic, crushed
juice of 1 lemon
water

1. Preheat oven to 350°.
2. Mix beef, seasonings, pine nuts and herbs together.
3. Combine tahini, garlic, lemon juice and enough water to make a thin sauce; pour over meat mixture.
4. Place mixture in individual casserole dishes and bake until meat is cooked and top is browned (about 45 minutes).

# MISSISSIPPI MOMMA'S MEAT LOAF

serves 6–8

3 pounds ground meat (2½ pounds of
   ground chuck or sirloin and ½ pound
   of pork ground together; no fat)
4 cloves garlic, chopped
2 medium size onions, chopped fine
2 green peppers, coarsely chopped
1 egg, beaten
½ teaspoon oregano
4 cups cubed bread or prepared bread
   stuffing
salt and pepper to taste
¾ cup milk
1 8-ounce can tomato sauce

1. Preheat oven to 350°.
2. Mix all ingredients, adding milk and half
   of tomato sauce last.
3. Shape mixture into a round loaf,
   resembling a bread loaf.
4. Grease bottom and sides of an iron skillet,
   place loaf inside and cover with remaining
   half of tomato sauce.
5. Place in oven for 1½ hours.

# ROBERT'S RUBBED GARLIC STEAK

serves 6–8

coarse salt to taste
3 cloves garlic, crushed
1 top sirloin or triangle tip roast (3–4
    pounds)
¾ cup prepared mustard
½ cup dry vermouth
salt and pepper to taste

1. Preheat oven to 475°.
2. Cover bottom of a heavy iron skillet with
   coarse salt and heat on top of stove.
3. Rub garlic into steak and brown on all
   sides.
4. Remove from pan and cover with mustard.
5. Return steak to skillet, add vermouth and
   bake for 20 minutes (or, using a meat
   thermometer inserted into thickest part of
   meat, until gauge registers 150° for
   medium rare).
6. Add salt and pepper; serve immediately.

# CRAZY JERRY'S PORK AND SHRIMP

serves 4

12-ounce package of fine noodles
1 tablespoon vegetable or peanut oil
2 cloves garlic, crushed
1 onion, sliced thin
1 pound pork, cut into ½-inch cubes, fat
    removed
½ pound small shrimp, cooked
salt and pepper to taste
chopped parsley
bacon bits

1. Cook noodles in 2 quarts boiling salted
   water until tender; drain thoroughly.
2. Heat oil in a heavy skillet and sauté garlic
   and onion until partially cooked.
3. Add pork; when almost cooked, add
   shrimp, salt and pepper.
4. When shrimp are warm, add noodles;
   stir-cook until heated.
5. Place on a warm platter and garnish with
   chopped parsley and crisp bacon bits.

# THE FLORENTINE PIG

serves 4–6

*You can serve this dish hot, but the Florentines love it cold.*

      8 ribs loin of pork
      3 cloves garlic, slivered
      ½ teaspoon dried rosemary
    2½ teaspoons salt
      ¾ teaspoon freshly ground pepper
      2 cups water

1. Preheat oven to 350°.
2. Trim fat from pork and cut a few incisions in ribs.
3. Roll garlic in rosemary and insert into slits.
4. Rub pork with salt and pepper, and place in a shallow roasting pan filled with the water.
5. Roast for 3 hours. After pork browns, baste with liquid every 20 minutes.

# CHICKEN LIVERS AL JEREZ

serves 4

1 onion, chopped fine
4 cloves garlic, chopped fine
1 tablespoon oil
1 pound chicken livers
¼ cup dry sherry
handful of chopped parsley

1. Sauté onion and garlic in oil until brown.
2. Add livers, sherry and parsley; sauté until
   livers are cooked.

## NOTE

If a thicker sauce is desired, add cornstarch;
if a thinner one, add a bit of water and more
sherry.

## VARIATIONS

Prepared kidneys or sweetbreads may be
substituted for the chicken livers.

from *Provence* by
FORD MADDOX FORD

I came yesterday, also in Fitzroy Street, at a party, upon a young lady who was the type of young lady I did not think one ever could meet. She was one of those ravishing and, like the syrens of the Mediterranean and Ulysses, fabulous beings who display new creations to the sound of harps, shawms and tea-cups. What made it all the more astounding was that she was introduced to me as being one of the best cooks in London—a real *cordon bleu,* and then some. She was, as you might expect, divinely tall and appeared to appear through such mists as surrounded Venus saving a warrior. But I found that she really could talk, if awfully, and at last she told me something that I did not know—about garlic. . . .

As do—as *must*—all good cooks, she used quantities of that bulb. It occurred to me at once that this was London and her work was social. Garlic is all very well on the bridge between Beaucaire and Tarascon or in the arena at Nîmes amongst sixteen thousand civilized beings. . . . But in an *atelier de couture* in the neighborhood of Hanover Square! . . . The lady answered mysteriously: No: there is no objection if only you take enough and train your organs to the assimilation. The perfume of *allium officinale* attends only on those timourous creatures who have not the courage as it were to wallow in that vegetable. I used to know a London literary lady who had that amount of civilization so that when she ate abroad she carried with her, in a hermetically sealed silver container, a single clove of the principal ingredient of *aioli.* With this she would rub her plate, her knife, her fork and the bread beside her place at the table. This, she claimed, satisfied her yearnings. But it did not enchant her friends or her neighbors at table.

My instructress said that that served her right. She herself, at the outset of her professional

136

career, had had the cowardice to adopt exactly that stratagem that, amongst those in London who have seen the light, is not uncommon. But when she went to her studio the outcry amongst her comrades, attendants, employers, clients and the very conductor of the bus that took her to Oxford Circus had been something dreadful to hear. Not St. Plothinus nor any martyr of Lyons had been so miscalled by those vulgarians.

So she had determined to resign her post and had gone home and cooked for herself a *poulet béarnais,* the main garniture of which is a kilo—2 lb—of garlic per chicken, you eat the stewed cloves as if they were *haricots blancs.* It had been a Friday before a Bank Holiday, so that the mannequins at that fashionable place would not be required for a whole week.

Gloomily, but with what rapture internally, she had for that space of time lived on hardly anything else but the usually eschewed bulb. Then she set out gloomily towards the place that she so beautified but that she must leave for ever. Whilst she had been buttoning her gloves she had kissed an old aunt whose protests had usually been as clamant as those of her studio-mates. The old lady had merely complimented her on her looks. At the studio there had been no outcry, and there too she had been congratulated on the improvement, if possible, of her skin, her hair, her carriage. . . .

She had solved the great problem; she had schooled her organs to assimilate, not to protest against, the sacred herb. . . .

This delightful story illustrates an important point about garlic: its taste changes more from the manner in which it is used than from the quantity. The beautiful model had not really trained her body to assimilate garlic better; rather she had treated the bulb in the most tender way possible. By using it whole, by not cutting into it and releasing its bite, she had tamed it. It became a fragrant complement to the dish, while retaining its anonymity.

Here follow two recipes for chicken: one like the already mentioned *poulet béarnais,* the other an American variation. Both use at least 40 cloves of garlic and are the best way to find out for yourself how beautifully this vegetable can be turned into an herb.

# POULET À L'AIL

serves 4

3–3½ pound roasting chicken
salt and pepper to taste
juice and peel of ½ a lemon
40 cloves garlic, peeled but not cut
1 bay leaf
3 parsley stalks
1 sprig each rosemary, thyme and sage
1 lump butter or 2 teaspoons oil
additional butter or oil
fresh parsley for garnish

1. Preheat oven to 350°.
2. Dry chicken, season insides with salt, pepper and lemon juice and truss.
3. Sauté garlic and herbs lightly in small amount of oil.
4. Remove herbs and place inside chicken with pieces of lemon peel.
5. Place garlic cloves on bottom of a roasting pan, place chicken on its side and coat with additional butter or oil. Cover with paper or well-fitting lid, place in oven and roast for about 15 minutes. Turn chicken over and roast another 15 minutes, covered. Remove covering and place chicken breast up. Bake for about a half hour, or until chicken is tender and browned, basting often.
6. Pour pan juices over chicken and serve garnished with garlic cloves and fresh parsley.

138

# CHICKEN À LA GARLIC

serves 6

6 chicken breasts, whole or halved
vegetable oil
salt and pepper to taste
1 teaspoon sage
3 pounds eggplant, cut in ¾-inch strips
2 onions, sliced thin
2 cups dry white wine
2 ounces brandy
40 cloves garlic, peeled but not cut

1. Preheat oven to 400°.
2. Brown chicken breasts in oil until lightly browned on all sides. Drain and put aside.
3. Sauté eggplant over low flame until browned but still firm. Season and set aside.
4. Sauté onions until browned and set aside.
5. Mix wine and brandy together and combine with any oil remaining in skillet.
6. In a large casserole, place garlic cloves on bottom; then alternate vegetables and chicken and add wine combination.
7. Bring to a boil on the stove; then bake, covered, for 1 hour and 45 minutes.

NOTE

Garlic can be served with chicken or spread on crackers; for those hesitant to indulge, there is still the wonderful fragrance it gives the chicken.

# THE GREAT GARLIC AND LEMON CHICKEN

serves 4

1 chicken, for broiling, cut into eighths
juice of 3 lemons
3 cloves garlic, crushed
pinch of oregano
salt and pepper to taste

1. Broil chicken pieces on both sides until juice begins to run out.
2. Meanwhile, combine lemon juice, garlic and seasonings.
3. Pour one-quarter of sauce over chicken and continue broiling.
4. Broil for approximately 40 minutes, or until chicken is thoroughly cooked and browned on both sides, adding sauce every 15 minutes. Reserve some sauce.
5. Place chicken in a bowl and pour remaining sauce over it. Cover and let stand for 10 or 15 minutes before serving.

# COLD "HOT" CHICKEN

serves 4–6

    1 3–4 pound frying chicken
    salt and freshly ground pepper to taste
    2 cloves garlic, cut in halves
    2 sprigs fresh tarragon
    1 sprig fresh rosemary
    pinch of thyme
1½ teaspoons curry powder
    1 small bay leaf
    1 cup peanut oil
    1 onion, cut in chunks
    1 clove garlic, sliced fine

1. Preheat oven to 450°.
2. Season chicken outside and in cavity with salt and pepper.
3. Combine herbs and curry powder and about 1 teaspoon of the oil and fill cavity.
4. Truss chicken with string or skewers.
5. Heat remaining oil in a large frying pan and fry chicken, onion and garlic until almost brown; then place in oven and bake for 15 minutes, basting frequently.
6. Turn chicken over and bake an additional half hour, until brown and tender.
7. Cool at room temperature and then refrigerate.

## TOPOLSKI'S GARLIC AND PAPRIKA PORK LOIN

serves 6

1 6-pound loin of pork
3 cloves garlic, quartered lengthwise
2 large carrots, cut into 8 strips
6 tablespoons butter
6 tablespoons olive oil
½ cup white wine
 salt and pepper to taste
½ teaspoon paprika
½ cup milk

1. Preheat oven to 325°.
2. Using a sharp knife, make incisions all around the pork and insert garlic; pierce the meat and insert carrot strips.
3. Heat butter and oil in an ovenproof dish, add pork and sauté over high heat browning on all sides.
4. Add wine and seasonings; when wine has evaporated, add milk.
5. Bake for about 1½ hours, basting and turning frequently.
6. When pork is done, slice into chops, arrange on platter and pour remaining sauce over pork.

# CASSOULET

serves 8

*This is a famous French peasant dish without which a book about garlic would be sadly lacking. It is so-named because the clay pot it was cooked in comes from the town of Issel:* cassol d'Issel.

    2 pounds dried navy or pea beans
    2 quarts salted water
    4 cloves garlic, cut in half
    2 carrots, cut in quarters
    2 onions, stuck generously with cloves
    1 bunch tied herbs (bay leaf, thyme,
        parsley)
    ½ pound salt pork or bacon
    1 pound boneless lamb, cubed
    3 onions, chopped
    2 tomatoes, cubed fine
2½ cloves garlic
    4 cups stock
    1 roasted duck or turkey (goose is most
        authentic, if available)
    1 pound garlic sausage
    breadcrumbs

1. Soak beans for 6 hours in salted water **or** boil quickly and soak for 1 hour.
2. Preheat oven to 300°.
3. Add cut garlic, carrots, onions, herbs and salt pork or bacon. Cook covered over low heat for an hour; skim top and remove herbs.
4. Brown lamb; add onions and tomatoes and 2 garlic cloves (crushed with a knife) and fry until onions are golden. Add stock and simmer slowly for 15 minutes.
5. Rub the bottom of a deep earthenware pot with half clove garlic, place a layer each of duck, sausage, salt pork, lamb and beans (beans should be the uppermost layer). Pour stock over all layers and springle some breadcrumbs on top. Bake, uncovered, until beans are cooked, but not dried out; this should take about an hour. Serve immediately.

143

Garlic has been revered as a folk medicine over the ages. It is a homeopathic remedy which has proven valid in some cases. Like any home remedy, it is not foolproof and you should rely on your physician for any medical treatments.

# THE GARLIC MEDICINE CHEST

66 . . . our doctor is a good clove of Garlic. 99

*A Deep Snow,* 1615

66 Garlic provokes urine and women's courses
(menses), helps the biting of mad dogs and other
venomous creatures, kills the worms in children,
purges the head, helps the lethargy, is a good
preservative against and remedy for any plague,
sore and foul ulcers, takes away spots and blemishes
in the skin, eases pain, ripens and breaks
impostumes (abscesses) or other swellings. 99

NICHOLAS CULPEPER

66 Garlic then have power to save from death.
Bear with it though it maketh unsavoury breath
And scorn not garlic like some that think,
It only maketh men wink and drink and stink. 99

SIR JOHN HARRINGTON, *"Englishman Doctor"* 1609

## DYSENTERY, AND OTHER INTESTINAL AILMENTS

"He [Bob Brown in Paris] was experimenting with visual verse in the Apollinaire tradition, and trying to cure with French beer the amoebic dysentery he had caught in South America. Poor Bob! Beer didn't do the trick; he had to go to Hamburg, to the Hospital for Tropical Diseases and take their famous 'Garlic Cure.' On his return, he described how he sat next to Sam Putnam and they told each other stories while the garlic juice was flushed through their intestinal canals three times a day."

WALTER LOWENFELS, *To An Imaginary Daughter* (New York: Horizon Press, 1964)

Despite the inevitable controversy surrounding garlic as treatment, there appears to be general agreement among most medical practitioners as to its benefits as a vermifuge—a destroyer of intestinal worms.

Dioscorides, the Greek physician who served in Nero's army and who was the first to establish a science from medical botany, wrote the important *Materia Medica* which prescribed garlic for all intestinal (and lung) diseases. So did Hippocrates.

Many physicians use garlic for treating gas, dyspepsia and diarrhea. One doctor used a garlic preparation in his practice for intestinal disorders in the following manner: For dysentery, 2 grams of the garlic preparation three times a day for three months; then 2 grams two times a day. For dyspepsia, 2 grams three times a day. (Most garlic perles are sold in grains; 1 gram = 15.433 grains.)

It is important to note that when using garlic one suffers none of the possible side effects of actual drugs.

I have had experience with the efficacy of garlic as a preventive for dysentery on the following regimen: 2 garlic perles three times a day for ten days prior to visiting an area where one might be susceptible. Garlic seems to have the ability to build up the intestinal flora—the healthy bacteria—while destroying the harmful kind. For these purposes, raw garlic is preferable; as well as perles or enemas. A Russian scientist in 1954 wrote of his experiments with garlic in this regard. Introducing the juice directly into colonies of harmful bacteria, he found that all movement stopped within three minutes and there was no activity whatsoever after ten minutes; freshly prepared juice was most effective.

A child was suffering from worms and advice was given to put some garlic cloves in the child's shoe. As he walked, the garlic was crushed and within a half hour it could be detected on his breath, attesting to the fact that it had penetrated his body and reached the lungs (as well as the intestines).

If you have a dog that needs deworming, perhaps you'd like to try this natural way. Mix garlic with dog's food. Even if it doesn't work, your dog will be happy; they love the taste of garlic (and fleas and tics hate it; it's good as a spray and far less toxic).

# RESPIRATORY AILMENTS

Garlic has been used to treat a whole spectrum of respiratory ailments from the plague to the common cold. European garlic was an early official entry in British and American pharmacopoeia for respiratory infections, parasites and as an aid in digestion.

During one of the great plagues which scourged seventeenth-century England a "miraculous" event took place. The occupants of one house in the area of Chester escaped completely from the disease, although they were in direct contact with those dying from it. The only explanation: a large supply of fresh garlic in the cellar. The house was named "God's Provident House" and became a public landmark.

Perhaps you've heard of or tasted a French vinegar called *Vinaigre des Quatre Voleurs* ("Four Thieves Vinegar"). According to one story, it originated in 1721 when Marseilles was prey to a plague even worse than England's. It became practically impossible to find people willing to bury the thousands of dead and the government was forced to release four convicts from prison to do the job. Despite their continuous exposure, none of the men showed any signs of the fatal disease and remained surprisingly healthy. The government officials were so astonished that they offered the men amnesty in exchange for the secret of their immunity. Simple: Every day the men drank wine in which a great quantity of fresh garlic was soaked. Through the years, vinegar was used instead of wine but the formula is credited to the thieves.

Colds have been treated with garlic in a variety of ways: at the onset, instead of rushing for the Coricidin, peel and cut a few cloves and inhale them several times a day (see page 152 for details); or hold a cut clove on the

148

side of the mouth between the cheek and teeth for as long as it burns—then hold another! In former days, children could be seen wearing necklaces of strung garlic cloves; sometimes they even had the soles of their feet rubbed with it to ward off contagious diseases and colds. At least one doctor found garlic the best cure for whooping cough and was brave enough to present it to his derisive colleagues at a medical meeting. What he did was to chop garlic cloves fine, using enough to make a ¼-inch poultice when placed between the thickness of soft cloth, he then oiled the soles of his patient's feet to prevent blistering (garlic oil can be very irritating to the skin) and bound the poultice on, finally putting on a sock to prevent slipping. The patient wore it overnight, and in the morning when it was removed, the garlic could be detected on his breath, indicating that it had traveled to the lungs. Not only was the treatment effective—it was exceedingly cheap; the same poultice could be used several times!

Tuberculosis, bronchitis and diptheria have all been treated with garlic; sometimes combined with honey. An English physician named Dr. Bowles devised a "secret" remedy for his asthma sufferers. He made a preserve of cut garlic cloves, vinegar and sugar which he kept in an earthen jar and administered together with a bulb or two (!) of garlic each morning while fasting.

During a flu epidemic in Russia in 1965 an emergency supply of 500 tons of garlic was rushed to the area and the *Evening Moscow Journal* advised people to consume more garlic than usual because of its "prophylactic qualities for preventing flu."

## HYPERTENSION, HIGH BLOOD PRESSURE

Garlic is equally respected as a treatment for high blood pressure and hypertension. The ancients used it often in treating symptoms of aging, primarily hardening of the arteries. Garlic appears to have some effect in relaxing the involuntary muscles and dilating the capillaries. In experiments on animals and humans there was significant vasodilation in peripheral blood vessels and some relief of hypertension.

## SOME RECIPES FOR TREATMENTS USING GARLIC

**SYRUP**—Peel 1 pound cloves, grind in a meat grinder and put in a large jar. Cover with equal parts of pure vinegar and distilled water. Shake well and let stand 4 hours. Strain. Add equal part hot syrup of brown sugar or honey. Seal and keep in a cool place.
DOSE—Adults—1 tablespoon 3 or 4 times a day
Children—1 teaspoon 3 times a day
USED FOR—coughs, asthma

**GARLIC OIL**—Peel ½ pound of cloves and mince. Cover with warm olive oil, shake and let stand in a warm place for 2 or 3 days. Strain through muslin, bottle and keep cool.
USED FOR—*ulcers:* 1 teaspoon 3 or 4 times a day
*earache:* warm a small amount and place 4 or 5 drops in ear; cover with flannel and keep warm
*athlete's foot:* wash feet well in hot soapy water and apply oil 2 or 3 times a day
*chapped hands:* rub in liberally
NOTE: To remove odor, add a few drops of oil of anise, caraway or cinnamon.

**GENERAL DRINK**—Grate or crush 3 or 4 cloves into a glass of very hot water, allow to stand overnight. Drink upon awakening. If stomach reacts unfavorably, begin with ½ clove and increase gradually.
USED FOR—circulatory problems, arterial tensions, cancers and precancerous conditions

**GENERAL TONIC**—3 cloves to 1 cup simmering milk on green salad or spread on hot toast. Only use for 10 days in spring or fall.
USED FOR—worms and parasites (Many Frenchmen take the "garlic cure" with new butter in the spring.)

151

## THIN SLICES OF CLOVES ON BUTTERED TOAST

USED FOR—loose teeth, inflamed tonsils and glands, laryngitis

### WITH A GLASS OF MILK

USED FOR—high blood pressure

### MIXED WITH GIN

USED FOR—rheumatism sufferers (also kills taste). In 1897, a Dr. Fernie advised making a medicinal tincture with wine.

DOSE—10–20 drops in water several times daily

**PALATABLE GARLIC JUICE**—30 garlic cloves, peeled, and 3 lemons with peel (seeds removed) cut in thin slices. Combine with 2 pints water, and mix in blender. Slowly heat and boil for a few minutes. Cool and strain; sweeten with honey.

DOSE—2–3 tablespoons daily, 2 hours before or after meals

For purposes of treatments, powdered garlic or garlic salt is not recommended. Many food values (as well as taste) are lost in the dehydrating process. Some people feel that garlic is most effective when chewed "straight," or with fruit or bread, to get the full benefit of the oil.

**A VAPOR**—Put finely chopped garlic on a dish or even just a piece of paper and while resting, inhale its odor for a few minutes at a time.

USED FOR—General cleansing of the blood-stream and detoxification.

## SKIN CONDITIONS

"Let it be taken inwardly with moderation; outwardly you may be more bold with it."
Anonymous

Raw garlic has been used to treat all manner of skin problems, though it must be pointed out that direct application of the strong oil may be irritating to the skin—oil or vaseline can be used as a good buffer.

### INSECT BITES AND STINGS

- The Dakota and Winnebago Indians applied crushed bulbs of wild garlic and onion to relieve the pain of bites and stings.
- Garlic has been chewed to keep mosquitoes and wasps away.
- Mohammed claimed that garlic produced soothing results when applied to scorpion and viper bites. Despite his objections (see page 102) he reportedly said, "If I did not have to speak with Gabriel, I would eat much garlic."
- Garlic has been used for snake bites and anthrax in cattle.

**POISON IVY**—Use a garlic poultice on the affected area (see whooping cough poultice, page 149).

**CALLOUSES AND CORNS**—Cut slices of garlic to fit the corn or callous and fix in place with adhesive overnight. This treatment also can be used for warts.

A garlic facial? Why not? (If you can take it.) Pimples have been known to shrink and fade away when rubbed with the powerful clove, and it's said that eaters of much garlic have healthy, good complexions.

# THE SUBJECT OF ODOR

"And, most dear actors, eat no onions nor Garlic, for we are to utter sweet breath."

SHAKESPEARE,
*"A Midsummer Night's Dream"*

One of the main objections garlic-haters have to the herb is its offensive aftertaste and smell, which they feel makes it an item of food appropriate only for hermits. There are some purported remedies for this problem—a few quite fanciful. Unfortunately even the most scientific cure will fail to work if one indulges heavily in garlic; for the smell cannot be thwarted by superficial measures, it penetrates the lungs and is therefore released with each exhalation. Nevertheless . . .

- The particles left in the mouth are to blame for the smell; rinse the mouth well with water and salt.
- Mince the garlic fine and swallow without chewing; put it in a teaspoon and place it as far back on the tongue as possible, then swallow it with some water.
- Chew one of the following with the garlic or immediately afterward: raw parsley, mint or other fresh green herbs, roasted coffee beans, orange peel, cardamon or caraway seeds, apples.
- Eat the garlic immediately before going to sleep.
- Instead of raw garlic, use garlic perles or pills that contain extract of garlic oil—some are combined with deodorizers like parsley or watercress.
- Buy empty size 00 gelatin capsules in a pharmacy. Chop a small clove of garlic and put it into a capsule. Make sure that the capsule is rinsed in cold water before swallowing it, and take one in the morning on an empty stomach.

- Use a garlic press to exclude the fibrous part of the garlic that causes the aftertaste.
- Unless the body is full of acid and congestion, garlic will not cause one to have an offensive breath.
- One quarter of a teaspoon bicarbonate of soda in half a glass of water once a day.
- Upon waking, make a mixture of salt, bicarbonate of soda and powdered borax. Place it in your palm and sniff it into your nose and out of your mouth.
- Get all your friends to eat garlic and nobody will notice!

"The offensiveness of the breath of him that hath eaten garlick will lead you by the nose to the knowledge thereof."
NICHOLAS CULPEPER

Nevertheless, the smell is important. Diallyl disulphide, the component responsible for the odor of garlic, is considered by many to also be responsible for its value, and for this reason, the most potent-smelling raw garlic is often recommended.

- Virile bacilli, that can be killed only after three hours of boiling, died after only an hour of exposure to garlic fumes in experiments in test tubes under different conditions than those that exist in the human body.

- Garlic juice combined with water—10 to 20 percent fresh garlic; an easy mixture made in a blender and then strained—can be sprayed on vegetables, fruits and other plants; it makes a harmless insecticide and helps to control plant diseases. The spray can be made to smell better by the addition of alpha neutroleum, a synthetic oil. Also, planting garlic near growing vegetables tends to discourage destructive bugs and insects.

*The Wall Street Journal* reported that two garlic-derived chemicals were 100 percent effective in laboratory experiments in killing larvae of several species of mosquito and other pests such as house flies, but these chemicals are nontoxic to higher animals. Natural and synthetic versions in concentrations as low as five parts per million effectively killed the larvae of one type of common mosquito.

## MISCELLANY

Got a toothache? Stick a clove of garlic in your ear. Got an earache? Do the same thing, only this time heat it slightly and cover your ear with a piece of flannel. Got a hangover? Do like the French, drink *Soupe à Lyvriogne* —made with garlic and onions.

One man claimed that he grew an abundant crop of hair after rubbing garlic over his bald spots three times a day.

Aristophanes swore garlic would restore "masculine vigor."

At the end of the eighteenth-century a Russian writer named Novokov published detailed advice on nursing babies. One suggestion guaranteed to facilitate weaning: smear the mother's or wet nurse's breast with garlic.

A Japanese scientist named Fujiwara claimed that the sulphur substance in garlic helped the body to assimilate the important vitamin B1 (thiamin).

Dr. Albert Schweitzer treated cholera and typhus with garlic. Hemorrhoids have been greatly relieved by insertion of a peeled clove, lubricated first.

Rheumatism and sciatica can be treated with a mixture of two parts oil to one part garlic rubbed into the affected area.

As already noted, garlic is a powerful antibiotic. As such it has played its part during wartime. The Russians used garlic in both world wars in much the same way as penicillin without any noticeable aftereffects or reactions; it was so sought after by the British government during World War II that they even advertised in order to secure an ample supply. It was found that when garlic was used in time, the incidence of gangrene and septic poisoning from wounds was significantly reduced.

Garlic is prominent among the controversial treatments for cancer. Some scientists have concluded that allicin, the bactericide in garlic, can inhibit the growth of enzymes in tumor cells; and a group of medical researchers in the Midwest found that cancerous cells introduced into rats after saturation doses of garlic oil had no effect. Cases of arrest of precancerous conditions of the lip have been reported from topical application of a garlic paste.

Last but not least: If you don't want to use garlic on yourself, use it on your china: the juice is supposed to be a good glue because it contains mucilage.

## ...AND MAD DOGS, TOO!

A woman was bitten by a rabid dog and as no remedy was known at the time, she was thrown into a jail cell. By convenient coincidence, a strand of garlic bulbs happened to be hanging from the ceiling. In her raving state, she bit into the garlic, ate it and soon fell asleep. When she awoke, she was completely cured.

Whether or not this story is fictional, the Roman naturalist Plinius noted many years ago that garlic was an excellent treatment for the bite of mad dogs (as did Culpeper, see page 144), and it has been used with success to treat hydrophobia (rabies).

# INDEX

CREDITS


Photos: half-title page, pages
16, 34, 62, 63, 66, 74 by Eric Cato
Drawings: pages 9, 13, 150 by
Paul Jenkins
Drawings: title page, pages 15,
33, 52, 53, 65, 77, 97, 105, 121
by Ira Friedlander